THE
OXYRHYNCHUS PAPYRI
VOLUME XXXV

THE
OXYRHYNCHUS PAPYRI

VOLUME XXXV

EDITED WITH NOTES
BY
E. LOBEL, M.A.

Graeco-Roman Memoirs, No. 50

———

PUBLISHED FOR
THE BRITISH ACADEMY
BY THE
EGYPT EXPLORATION SOCIETY
2–3 DOUGHTY MEWS, LONDON W.C.I
1968

PRINTED IN GREAT BRITAIN
AT THE UNIVERSITY PRESS, OXFORD, BY VIVIAN RIDLER
PRINTER TO THE UNIVERSITY
AND PUBLISHED FOR
THE BRITISH ACADEMY
BY THE EGYPT EXPLORATION SOCIETY
2–3 DOUGHTY MEWS, LONDON, W.C.1
ALSO SOLD BY
BERNARD QUARITCH, 11 GRAFTON ST., NEW BOND ST., W.1
KEGAN PAUL, TRENCH, TRUBNER & CO., 38 GREAT RUSSELL ST., W.C.1

PREFACE

In this volume Mr. Lobel edits four papyrus manuscripts that concern or give new texts of lyric poetry, and eight which add to our knowledge of Old Comedy. The latter are principally ancient commentaries, which offer new citations as well as information of literary, historical, and antiquarian interest. It goes without saying that for the recognition of value in these pieces and for the assembling of them the learned world is, as usual, in debt to Mr. Lobel.

The general editors would like to express the Society's thanks to the Jowett Copyright Trustees for undertaking financial responsibility for the cost of publishing this volume. They are also grateful to Dr. John Rea for making the index, to the Oxford University Printer for exercise of his wonted care, and to the Cotswold Press for the collotype reproductions.

E. G. TURNER
T. C. SKEAT
Joint Graeco-Roman Editor

May 1968

CONTENTS

TEXTS

TABLE OF PAPYRI

[1] All dates are A.D.

LIST OF PLATES

Fr. 1   Frr. 2–3 vacant

```
        ]ματα τ[
        ]λχενω[
        ]..εϲτιν[
        ]πολλω.[
  5     ]πολλονπα[
        ]τηντου..[
        ]θρωπου[
        ]αν..[
        ]. πλο.[
 10     ]ιδηεγ[.].[
        ].χη χαιρε[
        ]ϲ υμνην [
        ].νοϲκλοπ.[
        ]ενεθλια[
 15     ]ϲ.ον απολλω[
        ]αυτωι απειλη[
        ].εριϲπα[
        ]μωντατ[
        ]ρπηνλαβ[
 20     ] ηδετριτη.[
        ]ρχηνδεε[
        ]φαιϲιτετυχ[
        ]. .[  ].[
```

Fr. 1 There are loose fibres in the upper part of this fragment and a rubbed patch towards the middle, so that decipherment here is uncertain and precarious.

2]λ starts close to the edge but α looks unacceptable   3]. ., scattered traces, possibly of the right-hand stroke of ω and the feet of ν   4 .[, the lower part of an upright descending below the line   6 ..[, prima facie γ written rather low, followed by the foot of an upright; perhaps a single η 9]., the tip of an upright with a dot to left   10].[, the foot of an upright, followed by a dot on the same level   11]., faint traces compatible with the loop of ρ   13]., the end of a stroke touching the middle of the left-hand side of ν   .[, the tip of an upright   14 Of α[only a trace of the loop on the line   15 After ϲ an upright descending below the line with ink, perhaps casual, to left of its foot   17]., a small loop level with the top of the letters; π acceptable   20 .[, the upper left-hand arc of a small circle level with the top of the letters   21 ν is slightly anomalous, but η would be even more so   23]. .[, the right-hand end of a cross-stroke, followed at an interval by the upper end of a stroke descending to right and this, beyond the gap, by a dot at the same level; perhaps three letters

Fr. 1 4 Ἀ]πολλων[is not attractive as an interpretation of the ink, the first upright of the presumed ν being inordinately extended below the line, but it is commended by the next line, which seems to contain Ἀ]πολλον πα[ῖ, part of the first verse of the first poem in the first book of Alcaeus (fr. 307).

10 ὠ]ιδή is acceptable, but I cannot verify it. It might be followed by ἐγ[έ]ν[ετο.

11 seq. ἀ]ρχή. What follows is the beginning of the second poem in the first book of Alcaeus (fr. 308). If the lemma was written out in full, κυλλαναϲομεδειϲϲεγαρμοιθυμο]ϲυμνην gives a line of 33 letters (without allowing for blank spaces). This line was visibly on the short side and below, in l. 22, the lemma, if written out in full, νυμφαιϲταιϲδιοϲεξαιγιοχωφαιϲιτετυχ(με-), gives 34 (or 36) letters. Again, in fr. 6, since the τ of τα is exactly under the τ of το, the equivalent of a line falls between them, and τομενγαρενθενκυμακυλινδεταιτοδενθεν is equivalent to a line of 35 letters. There is thus a fair prima facie case for postulating a column about 35 letters wide. This is a good deal more than in **2306, 2307**, even if allowance is made for ἔκθεϲιϲ of one or two letters in the case of lemmata.

13 seqq. There are to be faintly descried in these remnants details known from other sources of the contents of Alcaeus' poem on Hermes: γ]ενεθλια[, a reference to his birthday (l. 14); κλοπή[, κλ]οπήν, to the theft of Apollo's oxen (and bow and arrows?) (ll. 13, 19); αὐτῶι ἀπειλή[ϲαϲ, to Apollo's threats (l. 16).

17 It is hardly questionable that some part of περιϲπᾶν is to be recognized and it is tempting to see a reference to the difference of opinion about the interpretation of μέδειϲ recorded by Apoll. Dysc. π. ϲυντ. 92b. But if I am right about the character of the work represented by these scraps, we are not to expect grammatical comments, and the position of the word, apparently in the middle of an account of the contents of the poem (if κλ]οπήν is rightly supplied in l. 19), is not in favour of the hypothesis. On the other hand, it is difficult to see to what detail of the story (as related in schol. *Il.* xv 256) περιϲπᾶν would be relevant, for though it is found in the sense of 'rob', I am inclined to doubt whether it could be used of the filching of the bow.

20 seqq. The 'third' (presumably, poem of the first book) is now revealed as having been that beginning with the line Alc. fr. 343.

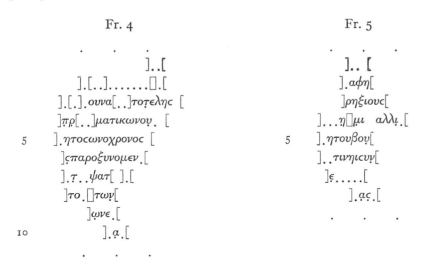

Fr. 4　　　　　　　　　　　　　　　　　Fr. 5

Fr. 4 The surface has been eaten off in a number of places

1 The top of an upright, followed by the lower part of a stroke descending below the line　2 The bases of letters　].[, the foot of an upright　After the gap a ligature to the top of an upright of which the lower part is preserved, followed by the feet of two more uprights; next, a large right-hand hook on the line, resembling the left-hand element of ω but not, I think, to be combined with

the following base of a small circle, off the line and having a dot to its right, which seems likely by itself to represent *o*; next, the feet of two strokes rising with a slight slant to right, followed by the lower left-hand, and this by the lower right-hand, arc of a circle, the base of a small circle off the line with a trace to its right, and, after a gap in which no whole letter may be lost, the top of an upright with a trace to its left   3].[, traces compatible with the top and the foot of ε   ]., two dots, one above, the other below, the general level   4 .[, I cannot interpret the ink, which looks like ϲ, written below the general level, with the foot of an upright, ascending above the general level, at its top left-hand corner; apparently not κ   5]., the right-hand side of a loop, as of ρ   6 Of]ϛ only the end of the top stroke and the foot; ε possible   .[, perhaps a middle stop intended   7]., the top of a tall upright   Between τ and ψ perhaps ερ, but the ε anomalous and a dot above the line between ρψ not accounted for   8 After *o* a dot level with the top of the letters   10]., the right-hand edge of the upper right-hand arc of a circle   .[, the thickened top of an upright

Fr. 5 The left-hand side is rubbed in ll. 4–6, the surface partly stripped in ll. 7–8

1 The bottom right-hand arc of a circle close to the lower part of an upright descending well below the line   2]., the right-hand edge of a small circle level with the top of the letters; ρ acceptable   4]..., an upright, followed at an interval by the top of an upright sloping slightly forward and this by a shorter stroke with more slope, apparently ligatured to η and perhaps representing δ or λ   If η and μ are rightly recognized no whole letter is lost in the gap between them, but for μ perhaps α should be substituted   .[, a short horizontal stroke to right of the top of ι   5]., the lower end of a stroke descending from left and the top of an upright slightly to right of it; ν suggested, but it is not the usual ν of this hand   Of υ[only the foot, but the spacing supports it   6].., an upright concave stroke with a ligature to its top, possibly ι   7 After ε apparently the top of δ or λ; next, the upper part of a rather angular oval not suggesting θ, rather large for *o*. The rest are indeterminate traces on a single fibre level with the top of the letters   8]., a dot on the line .[, an upright

Fr. 4 3 Ἀ[ριϲ]τοτέλης probable. ριϲ looks rather crushed, but I think this is due to the slightly incorrect adjustment of the two scraps of which the fragment has been made up.
     4 πρ[αγ]ματικῶν.

Fr. 6   Fr. 7

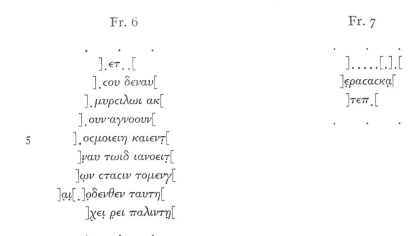

```
        .   .   .                    .    .    .
     ].ετ..[                      ].....[.].[
     ].ϲου δεναυ[                 ]ερασακα[
     ].μυρϲιλωι ακ[               ]τεπ.[
     ].ουν·αγνοουν[
  5  ].οϲμοιειη καιεντ[              .    .    .
     ]ναυ τωιδ ιανοειτ[
     ]ων ϲταϲιν τομενγ[
     ]αι[.]οδενθεν ταυτη[
     ]χει ρει παλιντη[

        .    .    .
```

Fr. 6 1]., two dots on the line; perhaps ν or π, but perhaps representing two letters   ..[, the base of a circle, followed by the lower part of an upright descending below the line and turning sharply to left; perhaps αι, but ι not so made elsewhere   2]., a ligature to the top of ϲ, preceded by

traces on frayed-out fibres; possibly ω   3]., a stroke rising to the upper left-hand stroke of μ
4]., the lower end of a stroke descending in a curve from left   5]., a dot on the line   7 Of
]ω only the ligature to ν   8 Of]ọ only traces on frayed-out fibres   9 Of]χ only the tips of the
upper arms

Fr. 6 3 seqq. *Μυρcίλωι*: from the commentary partly preserved in Alc. fr. **305** it is apparent that
the piece beginning with the verses recognizable in ll. 7 seq., below, which we learn from Heracl. *qu.*
Hom. 5 contains a hidden reference to Myrsilus, was preceded (in all likelihood, immediately) by
another piece relating to a service to the same Myrsilus performed by one Mnamon. I call attention,
therefore, to *ουδεναυ*[, l. 2, ∼ *οὐκ αἰτιᾶται αὐτὸν οὐδὲ διαφέρεται*, fr. 305 i 20, *Μυρcίλωι ἀκ*[, l. 3, ∼ *ἀκάτιον*
παρέcτηcεν εἰc τὴν Μυρcίλου κάθοδον, ib. 17 seqq.,].*οcμοιειη*, l. 5, ∼ *ἐ̣*[..]. *αμοι πόλεμοc μήτε γένοιτο*, ib.
14 seq., without seeing any way of testing the relevance of these comparisons.

4 (-)*π*]*λουν*.

4 seq. *κα*[*ταπ*]*λουν* and *μη*]*τεπο*[*λε*]*μοc* are possibilities perhaps worth mentioning, but I cannot
verify this location of fr. 7 by means of the cross-fibres.

7 seq. Alc. fr. **326**.

9 *ἐπι*]*χειρεῖ*.

Fr. 7 looks as if it must have stood near the middle of the left-hand side of fr. 6, but I have
failed to find any precise location. See fr. 6, 4 seq. n.

1]..., on the line the start of a stroke rising to right, followed by an angular loop and this by the
base of a circle at a slightly higher level. The remaining traces are only dots on a single fibre   3 .[,
on the line the lower part of a stroke apparently turning to right

Fr. 8 vacant

Fr. 9

```
   ·        ·      ·
]ταπραγμ[
]νεγενε[
  ]..[
   ·        ·
```

Fr. 10

```
   ·          ·
]ακαι[
]εαν[
].ι ο α[
].μεν .[
   ·      ·      ·
```

Fr. 9 3 A dot representing the top of a letter,
followed by what most suggests the upper part of
ξ, though unlike the others

Fr. 10 1 Or]ε? αι remade on α by the
original hand   3]αι probable   4]., a dot
in the middle position   .[, the left-hand arc of
a small circle in the middle position

Fr. 11

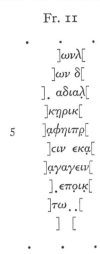

]ωνλ[

]ων δ[

]. αδιαλ[

]κηρικ[

5   ]αφηιπρ[

]cιν εκα[

]αγαγειν[

]. επρικ[

]τω .. [

] [

Fr. 11 Prima facie the bottom of a column.

3]., perhaps η or ν, perhaps ι with a ligature from a preceding α or the like   4 For η I am not sure that αι might not be substituted   5 Of]α only the right-hand stroke, but λ less likely 8]., on the line the foot of a stroke with a small hook to right   Of κ[only the upright; perhaps η 9 ..[, the apex of δ or λ, followed by the upper left-hand part of a loop as of ε

Fr. 11 3 If ἀδιάλ[ειπτο-, cf. Alc. fr. 305 i 13 seq. ἀνέκλειπτον πόλεμον ἕξετε. If this scrap is to be supposed to contain matter preceding that contained in fr. 6, it will have come from the bottom of the preceding column. There is no physical resemblance between them.

Fr. 12 (*a*)   Fr. 12 (*b*)

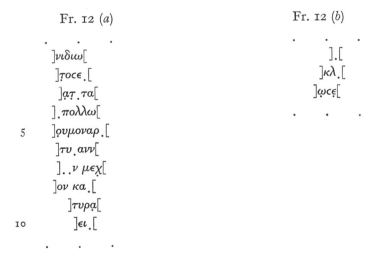

]νιδιω[   ].[

]τοcε.[   ]κλ.[

]ατ.τα[   ]ωcε[

].πολλω[

5   ]ουμοναρ.[

]τυ.ανν[

]..ν μεχ[

]ον κα.[

]τυρα[

10]ει.[

Frr. 12 (*a*), (*b*) have a strong general resemblance but I can establish no exact relation between them by means of the fibres of either side.

12 (*a*) 2 .[, the feet of two uprights, the second hooked to right, e.g. *ν*   3 Of *τ* the stalk has disappeared. To the right of its cross-stroke there appears to be a thin continuation, but there is now no other trace of ink between *τ* and *τ*   4]., the foot of an upright, below the line   5 .[, the start of a stroke rising to right   6 Between *υ* and *α* a damaged place with scattered traces, compatible with *ρ*   7].., the upper end of a stroke rising from left with a slightly convex stroke depending from its top; scattered traces below to right   10 .[, ink resembling the upper right-hand side of *ο* but with a projection curving forward from its top

Fr. 12 (*b*) 1 The lower part of an upright with a stroke diverging upwards from its foot; if one letter, a 'split' *τ*   2 .[, a short arc from the upper left-hand side of a circle

Fr. 12 (*a*) 5 μοναρχ[- Alc. fr. **6** (A 6) 27 μοναρχίαν.

6 τυρχνν[- Alc. fr. **75** (D 17) 13 τυραννεύ-, fr. **348** (Z 24) 3 τύραννον, fr. **302** (R 1 ii 11) τύρα[, fr. **179** (1̄1 40 ii 3) on καὶ τὸν μο[a schol. ¹].ονε|²]το( ) τυ|³ρα]ννίς. The word may recur in l. 9, below.

Fr. 13

.   .   .

].οηι.[

].ωνπα[

]..ιτυ[

].πολ[

5   ]ρ αγα[

]εϲπα[

].ϲμα[

.   .   .

Fr. 13. Frayed and rubbed. Many letters very dubiously deciphered.

1]., the upper end of a stroke about level with the top of the letters but sloping gently up to right. L. 2 begins with a similar stroke with a slightly more marked slope. *κ* not suggested in either place   3].., on the line the foot of a stroke hooked to right, e.g. *ν*, followed by a trace on the line and another above and to right   4]., an upright with a trace on the line to left; perhaps *ν* or *π*   7]., traces compatible with *ν*, but perhaps two letters,].ι

2735. Choral Lyric

Not much profit, that I see, is to be drawn from the collection of scraps printed under this number. It does not appear doubtful that they represent compositions to be described as choral lyric. Of the authors who employ the same (or a similar) conventional dialect in which they are written Simonides, Pindar, and Bacchylides may, I believe, be at once ruled out for the reason given at fr. 1, 11 n. Stesichorus and Ibycus are left of the major poets whose names we know and of this pair I should incline to Stesichorus, on the general ground that manuscripts of his poems have turned up in Oxyrhynchus many times more often than those of Ibycus (only **1790**+ **2081**(*f*)), and for the particular reason that there is a chance that fr. 11 has a connexion with the Ἄθλα ἐπὶ Πελίαι which Stesichorus wrote. These are weak arguments, but even if the authorship were established, what has survived is so discontinuous—palaeographical considerations make it reasonable to suppose that the fragments represent no small extent of writing, perhaps more than one manuscript— that it affords little or no information about subject or treatment, structure, or metre.

The hand is untypical and has a strongly marked character that makes it readily identifiable even in small quantities, although it displays wide variations in size and weight and a good deal of irregularity in the formation of some letters. Peculiarities of one kind or another are to be seen particularly in ε, ο, ϲ, τ, υ. As far as I can tell the lection-signs are mostly due to the writer of the text. So apparently are some of the marginalia, but in these two other hands are recognizable. I should guess the copy to have been made in the second century.

Fr. 1

```
                    .            .
                 ]τερεν .[
                        . [
                 ]εαπα[
            ]δ[   ]αριω[
        ] . δᾱκ . ονεχῳ[
 5      ] . λητηροσαειδο[
                 ]αβρὰπ[ . ]ντῶϲ[
        ] . οϲοίάτερωτοϲ[
                 ]ιοκαταιϲανώ.[
                 ]ατοντελοϲαϲφ[
10               ]αδυναμ̅ιϲ · κρατ[
        ] . νοιμεταδάι      [
        ]πολυνολβονὲδώκ[
                 ]ελωϲινέχεντοῖϲδα[
                 ]ιϲιμοιρᾶν ·        [
15               ]τυνδαρίδ[ ]ϲιλᾱγε[
        ] . ιϲαλπιγγοϲὸκενκε[
                 ]θιπποδαμωικαι . [
                 ]εϲαντὶθέοι         [
                 ]νοπᾱονεϲ · οἱϲινεϲ . [
20               ]ε̣ιμεγαλαχρύϲαιγιϲ[
                 ]καδέα .            [
        ] . ενουφατονεϲτινε[
                 ]ωντεκεεϲϲι · ϲεδᾱυ[
                 ]ενκαταδερκεται̣αι̣α[
25      . . ']τακαλλιϲτονεπιχθ[
        ]οιϲεναλ[ . ]γκιονειδο̣[
                 ]ϲαλλοϲουτῶϲ[] . . [
        ]ανιᾱοναϲουτ . [
        ]υδιανειρανα[ . ]ελ[
30      ] . δαιμονανα̈ο[
        ] . ϲτεχορο̑ιϲίππο̣[
        ]ᾶνβαθυνευ           [
        ]' . αμφιτεθαυμα[
        ] . λϲεαα̅χᾱ́εντε . [
35      ]πουϲ · ·λαχνᾱ[
        ]μοϲυνᾱιτεκαιδρ[
        ]ττᾶτ'εϲαγῶνεπᾱϲ[
        ]νπατερωνιδήρα[
        ]νια                [
40      ] . εθεω . [ . ]αρεϲτιδε[
        ]ε̣ϲϲα̣[ . . ¯]θεμιϲκα[
              ]            [
                    .   .   .
```

Fr. 1 1 .[, off the line the lower part of a slightly convex or forward-sloping stroke   2 Of]ϵ only the tip of the overhang and end of the cross-stroke   Above ą[, of which only the base of the loop, a v.l.   4]., the foot of a forward-sloping stroke   Of κ only the foot of the upright and the lower branch   The extreme right-hand end of a cross-stroke touches the top of ο   Of ω[only the top of the left-hand stroke   5]., level with the top of the letters, on a single fibre, part of a cross-stroke with a thickening at the right-hand end   7]., the middle part of a slightly concave stroke with the right-hand end of a cross-stroke through it; θ?   8 .[, the edge of a slightly convex upright having a projection to left of the top   11]., the lower end of an upright descending below the line and a horizontal stroke above it in the interlinear space   τ may be a badly made γ   12 Of]π̄ only a speck of the top right-hand corner   16]., the right-hand base angle of a triangle; anomalous for δ or φ, perhaps ο or ω   17 .[, γ or the left-hand part of π   19 .[, the edge of an upright   20 Of]ϵ only the right-hand extremities   21 Of]κ the same   Of ą only the base of the loop and the tip of the downstroke   22]., a trace on the line suggesting the lower end of a stroke descending from left   26 κ into γ!, first hand?   27] . .[, a small ο, followed at an interval by the lower part of a forward-sloping stroke with a dot above and to left; apparently part of a marginal note   28 .[, on the line a convex stroke, above it a concave stroke touching the end of the cross-stroke of τ; presumably τ᾽ followed by α or ο   29 Of]υ only the end of the right-hand branch   30]., on the line the end of a stroke descending from left   31]., the same   33].., the tip of an upright followed by a cross-stroke as of τ   34]., on the underlayer a stroke sloping from left to about mid-letter; α not suggested   .[, the lower part of a stroke rising to right   35 By the first hand, but anomalous   40]., the upper corner and cross-stroke of γ suggested, not τ   .[, an apex as of λ, but ν may be possible though the left-hand stroke would be more than usually sloping   41 The second c remade or written on another letter

Fr. 1 5 Archilochus is quoted for ἀίδων ὑπ᾽ αὐλητῆρος (fr. 123, perhaps at **2312** fr. 6, 8). Theognis has ὑπ᾽ αὐλητῆρος ἀείδειν (825; ἀκούων 533), μετ᾽ αὐλητῆρος ἀείδειν 1065.

6 παντῶς Doric accentuation Apoll. Dysc. π. ἐπιρρ. 170, 15. Similarly οὑτῶς, l. 27.

7 οἷά τε adverbial? Cf. Alcm. 56, 4, Bacchyl. v 65.

8 κατ᾽ αἶσαν 'rightly, rightfully', cf. *Il.* vi 333 κατ᾽ αἶσαν . . . οὐδ᾽ ὑπὲρ αἶσαν, Pind. *Pyth.* x 26 (schol. κατὰ τὸ προσῆκον), Bacchyl. x 32;)(οὐ κατ᾽ αἶσαν Pind. *Pyth.* iv. 107 (schol. παρὰ πάντα τὰ δίκαια), παρ᾽ αἶσαν *Pyth.* viii 13 (scholl. παρὰ τὸ καθῆκον, παρὰ τὸ δέον).

Or, if]ιο represents a genitive, cf. Pind. *Nem.* iii 15 οὐκ . . . Ἀριστοκλείδας τεὰν ('ἐάν') . . . κατ᾽ αἶσαν (schol. διὰ τὸ σὸν μέρος; κατὰ τὴν ἑαυτοῦ μερίδα . . ., ὅσον γε αὐτῶι ἀνῆκε).

I cannot account for the 'short'. The best guess I can make at the reading is ὡς.

10 δύναμις v.l. δύνασις. At Bacchyl. x 49 δύναμιν corrected to δύνασιν. δύνασις three times in Pindar (*Pythians*).

10 seq. Possibly κράτ[ος . . . μέγα.

11 seq. ἐδώκ- implics ἐδώκαν, Doric accentuation, and this makes δαίμονες a reasonably likely supplement, but I do not see why it should have been considered to require an accent.

ἐδώκαν and ν]ικάσαν fr. 11, 8, and likewise ἀντιθέοι, l. 18, and ἀγερώχοι fr. 27 (*b*) 14 are furnished with Doric accents. It must therefore be remarked that **2430**, which there is reason to attribute to Simonides, has other Doric characteristics but not this: ἄεισαν fr. 4 ii 8, ἔστᾱσαν fr. 32, 2,]βάρῡνον ibid. 4, and μεταιέμενοι fr. 35 (*b*) 9. On the other hand, manuscripts of Stesichorus,[1] when accented, have in these cases Doric accents, e.g. **2359** (Cυοθῆραι) ii 2 ἰζάνον, i 2 ὀψιγόνοι, ἀσπασί|οι, **2617** (Γηρυονηΐς) fr. 29, 3 ἠλύθον, fr. 1, 2 ἐχοίσαι, fr. 2, 2 ἀρίστοι.

13 ἔχεν i.e. ἔχειν, as at fr. 6, 3 seq. αειδεν, λεγεν. At **2430** fr. 79, 12 θόρέν (aorist). τοῖσδ᾽ α- seems to be implied.

15 Τυνδαρίδ[αι]σι, and so, l. 17, Κάστορι] θ᾽ ἱπποδάμωι καὶ . . . . λαγέ[ται in some form.

16 I should guess ὅκ᾽ ἐν κε[. I now believe that ὅκ᾽ for ὅτε should be recognized at **2430** fr. 47, 2.

17 On the analogy of Κάστορά θ᾽ ἱππόδαμον καὶ πὺξ ἀγαθὸν Πολυδεύκεα *Il.* iii 237, *Od.* xi 300 there is likely to be a mention of Polydeukes at the end of this verse, but whether π[stands for πύξ or Πω-, Πολυδεύκει (or some equivalent, e.g. Πολυδεύκεος βίαι as at Simon. fr. 4, 1) or something else, there is nothing to show.

[1] **1790** (+**2081** (*f*)), which preserves verse attributed to Ibycus, displays the same system as MSS. of Stesichorus.

18 seq. ἀντίθεος from Homer onwards regularly (though not uniquely) a qualification of nobles. Here perhaps ἥρω]ες ἀντιθέοι (as at Pind. *Pyth.* i 53, iv 58) 'and their . . . henchmen'.

20 χρύσαιγις at Bacchyl. fr. 15 of Athena, χρυσαίγιδος Ἰτωνίας (accented -γίδ- in the MSS., wrongly, see Chandler § 647).

21 As the accent shows, a compound of -καδής.

22 seqq. I should guess that the general sense might be: the children of the (gods) have ineffable (beauty). At any rate this seems to offer an acceptable antithesis to 23 seqq.

23 seq. cὲ δ' αὖ . . . καταδέρκεται. . . . Perhaps οὐρανόθ]εν and ἁ[(ε)λιος precede and follow. But *Od.* xi 15 seq., οὐδέ ποτ' αὐτούς | ἠέλιος φαέθων καταδέρκεται ἀκτίνεσσι, is a warning that the arrangement of the words may be different.

25 seq. ἐόν]τα κάλλιστον ἐπιχθ[ονίων . . . ἀθανάτ]οις ἐναλ[ί]γκιον εἶδο[ς will probably not do much injustice to the sense.

27 I suppose a negative is to be supplied: 'no other . . . so . . .', οὔτι]ς or the like.

28 seqq. It seems possible that the sense is: neither Ionian nor Lacedaemonian.

ἀν' Ἰάονας? For this use of ἀνά with people (instead of regions) the only precise parallel I can adduce is *Od.* xiv 286 ἀν' Αἰγυπτίους ἄνδρας.

If κ]υδιάνειραν, I think it looks more probable that the meaning is 'renowned in men' (though the only other instance would be *Anth. Plan.* 1, 2 (Cπάρτα κυδιάνειρα) than the Homeric 'where men gain renown' (of μάχη, ἀγορή).

Λακ]εδαίμονα ναίο[ντ-. There seems to be no reason to postulate (ἐ)ναίον.

34 seq. ἄλcεα. I am not certain about the purpose of the marginal additions, both by the original hand. The second is marked as a variant; the first looks as if it might be meant to carry on the line (which would then have to be transcribed ἄλcεα ἀχάεντ' ἐ.[), though for one reason or another it is at a lower level.

λαχνά[implies λαχνά -εις or -εντ⟨ˇ⟩ and might, I suppose, be an alternative reading to ἀχάεντα, but though ἄλcεα ἀχάεντα is comprehensible in the light of *Il.* xvi 765 seqq. (especially πρὸς ἀλλήλας ἔβαλον . . . ὄζους ἠχῆι θεσπεσίηι), the nearest parallel I can offer to ἄλcεα λαχνάεντα, 'shaggy groves', is λαχνήεντ' ὄροφον, *Il.* xxiv 451, referring to the 'rough' appearance of thatch. Oppian actually employs both λάχνη and λάχναι in the sense of 'foliage', *Halieut.* iv 167, 380. A different view of the matter might be, that there is no connexion between the marginal additions, that λαχνά[- is a variant for, say, χαιτά- and that either (completed -εντας) qualifies ἵπ]πους.

36 παλαι(c)]μοcύναι τε καὶ δρ[όμωι suggested; cf. Tyrt. 12, 2 οὔτε ποδῶν ἀρετῆς οὔτε παλαισμοcύνης.

37 ἐς ἀγῶν' ἐπ' Ἀc[ωπ-? Cf. Pind. *Nem.* iii 4, ix 9, *Pae.* vi 134.

38 ⟨ε⟩ἰδήρα[το-. Cf. Hesych. in ἰδήρατος· καλός, ὡραῖος. Not found elsewhere.

Fr. 2

```
            ·   ·     ·
        ]cε . . .[
        ]ωροπ.[
        ]μεγις.[
        ]μουπολ[.].[
   5    ]c              [
        ]νταφοινιοιcι.[
        ]              [
             ∪⊢  ·βέλ . . . ι·
        ]εναδινοιcβελεεcc[
        ]οcαργυροπεζου  [
  10    ]εγεντο.[
            ·   ·     ·
```

Fr. 2 1 After ε the left-hand arc of a circle off the line, followed by the foot of an upright turning sharply up to left; perhaps αι, ατ, or the like .[, a short arc from the lower left-hand side of a circle 2 Above ο traces, perhaps of ⊢ .[, an upright with a median trace to right; η? 3 .[, a speck on the line 4].[, a dot on the line 6 .[, the lower part of an upright 8 *sscr.* βέλεϲϲι to be presumed, but βέλεϲι may be possible 10 .[, the apex of a triangle

Fr. 2 3 μεγιϲτ[-.
4 Κάδ]μου πόλιϲ, or a derivative, in some case; a long shot.
6 φοίνιοϲ a rare word (once in the *Odyssey*, once in Pindar), except in the Tragedians.
8 ἁδινόν with a smooth breathing at Pind. *Pyth.* ii 53 (the only instance in lyric except Timoth. *Pers.* 29) and more often than not in MSS. of Homer. The rough breathing based on two theories: (*a*) παρὰ τὸ ἅδην ... διὸ καὶ δαϲύνεϲθαι αὐτό τινεϲ βούλονται καθὰ ἐν τοῖϲ Ἀπίωνοϲ καὶ Ἡροδώρου δηλοῦται Eust. 178, 22; similarly schol. *Il.* ii 87; (*b*) α before δ, except when privative or the result of a crasis, takes a rough breathing, schol. A *Il.* xi 88 (Herodian?).
9 ἀργυρόπεζοϲ known only from *Anth. Pal.* v 59 (Rufinus), where it is applied to a girl. Perhaps like ἀργυρόπουϲ it might be applied to a piece of furniture.

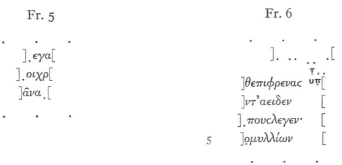

Fr. 3

    ].[
    ].α[
    ]ᾱν[
    ]ρυ.[
5].ᾰν[
    ]νῠ[

Fr. 4

]δακεθυμ[
].αϲπαιδῶ[

Fr. 3 1 An upright with the start of a cross-stroke going to right from its top. There is also a cross-stroke going to left from its foot, which does not look like a 'long' over α, l. 2 2]., the upper part of a stroke descending to right 3 Of the 'long' only the right-hand end 4 .[, the left-hand arc of a circle 5]., a trace level with the top of the loop of α

Fr. 4 There is a 'joint' at the right-hand edge
2]., a speck level with the top of the letters
Fr. 4 1 Cf. δακέθυμοϲ ἱδρώϲ Simon. fr. 74, 5.

Fr. 5

].εγα[
].οιχρ[
]ᾶνα.[

Fr. 6

]. .. .. .[
]θεπιφρεναϲ ὑπ[
]ντ'αειδεν   [
].πουϲλεγεν· [
5]ομυλλίων   [

Fr. 5 1]., the lower end of a stroke curving down from left to mid-letter   2]., a longer piece of a similar stroke touching *o* near its base   Above χ a dot, perhaps casual   3 .[, a slightly concave upright

Fr. 6 1]. . ., the lower left-hand arc of a circle, followed at an interval by two hooks to right on the line *Marg.* 1 . . .[, the lower part of a stroke curving up to right, followed by the lower part of an upright with a horizontal stroke to right from its top; at an interval the base of a circle 2 . .[, prima facie ηλ[, but this may be illusory   4]., possibly the bottom right-hand angle of *o*.

Fr. 6 5 I can make no better guess than that this represents a derivative of στωμύλος, but there is no doubt that]ω was not written. Diminutives in -ύλλιον are alien to lyric verse.

Fr. 7

].[
].ροςδρ[
].αἰμ[
]τουτ.[
5   ] μεγα.[
     ] ητομ.[
     ] cο..[
     ] ό[

Fr. 7 1 A thickened upright with the start of a cross-stroke to right of its top   2]., traces compatible with the right-hand upright of π, but not verifiable   Of ρ[only the upright   3]., apparently elements of an upright   4 .[, the middle part of the left-hand side of a circle? 5 .[, the top and bottom of an upright?   6 .[, the start of a stroke rising to right?   7 ..[, an upright, suggesting the left-hand stroke of ν, with a speck to right which could represent the tip of the right-hand stroke, followed by the apex of a triangle   8 In the left-hand margin an isolated dot

Fr. 8

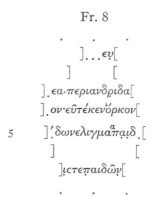

]...εν[
]   [
].εα·περιανδριδα[
].ον·εὗτέκενὄρκον[
5   ]′δωνελιγμᾶπαιδ.[
     ]   [
]ιcτεπαιδῶν[

Fr. 8 1]..., a dot on the line closely followed by the end of a stroke curving down from left and this by a hook like the base of c; next, two dots on the line, perhaps representing one letter   3]., on a single fibre a cross-stroke opposite the middle of ε   Between α and π a thin upright ending below in a thick dot and perhaps having a cross-stroke to right running into the top of π   4]., on the line a hook to right   5]., perhaps ι, but much damaged   .[, perhaps the edge of the left-hand arc of a circle

Fr. 8 4 εὗτέ κεν   Pindar εὗτ' ἄν (3 times) only. Neither elsewhere in lyric.

Fr. 9

. . .

]χ[.].[.].[
]ạτερειαθ̣[
]ηιπὸται.[
]αγοιϲ.̀[
].κωιερευθ[
]ν̣κελαδῆι.[
].ετετεκνạ[
]..ϲενϲτη̣[
]αταιδια[
]ạίδεραṭ[
]ονοῦκατα[
]νπροπο.[
].ηρ̣επεϲ[

. . .

Fr. 9 2 Of]ạ only the right-hand stroke Of θ̣[only the left-hand edge 3 .[, the upper and lower ends of the left-hand stroke of ν acceptable, but χ is an alternative and there are others 4 .[, the lower left-hand part of a circle; α, ο, ω apparently possible 5]., the lower end of a stroke descending from left 6 For]ν̣ perhaps ι .[, the bottom left-hand angle of δ? 7]., the edge of the right-hand arc of a circle? Of ạ[only the left-hand end of the loop 8].., the upper end of a stroke descending gradually to right, followed by traces compatible with the top and the end of the cross-stroke of ε Of η̣[only the first upright 10 Of]ạ only the tail. Above it what appears to be an upright; ʽ not suggested Of ṭ[only the left-hand end of the cross-stroke and the extreme lower end of the stalk 12 .[, a dot on the line, followed by the start of a stroke rising to right 13]., a speck just below the top of the letters

Fr. 9 2 εὐπ]ατέρεια.
3 ποταιν[ι-.

Fr. 10

. . .

] [
] [
]διταϲ [
].αν [
3].[

. . .

Fr. 10 2]., the lower part of an upright 3 The top of an upright

Fr. 11

]μιθεωνὁθ[

]. ἁδιονδρομ[

]π.νтαсαπλᾱτ.[

]χαλεπαδέτιсαλ[

5]ἄτεсιδᾰρεοсεπ[

]ρακλεοсγαμεν.[

]νυφαρμαсιτε[

]ι κᾱсαντρεχο[

]ᾰсϊο..οсαρηϊο.[

10]πιβᾱ.ταδεδε.[

]ηλευ[.]δεπαλα..[

]υδοсυπερτερον[

]ᾰμενουδυν[

]ᾱνανίκατο[

15]’δεκαιμε˙.[

]αικρατε.[

]χρῡсᾱο..[

]γαρυονανγ[

].τανεν.[

20]με..[

]αῑ.[

. . . .

Fr. 11 There is a 'joint' running irregularly down the middle

2]., the right-hand part of a cross-stroke touching the top of α   3 Of]π only the right-hand convex upright. It is followed by o or α, either anomalous   π made out of τ; λ retouched   .[, the middle part of the left-hand arc of a circle   4 Of]χ only the right-hand ends of the crossed strokes For λ[I am not sure that ν is not preferable   6 .[, the left-hand arc of a circle   9 Between o and o a dot on the line and a slightly backward-sloping upright   .[, the lower part of an upright 10 Between ά and τ a comma-like hook, level with the top of the letters, followed by the upper tip of a stroke descending to right; if these are to be combined, there is room for a narrow letter after   Of τ no sign of the left-hand part of the bar   .[, a dot level with the top of the letters   11 ..[, a dot off the line, followed by the lower left-hand arc of a circle   15]., the upper tip of a stroke rising from left   .[, the lower part of an upright descending below the line. Between this letter and ε something inserted above the line   16 Of ε only the upper left-hand part, but not, I think, o .[, a trace level with the top of the letters   17 o ex ι first hand   .[, a speck off the line, followed at an interval by the lower part of a stroke rising to right   18 Of]χ only the right-hand end of the cross-stroke   Of χ[the upright is anomalously sinuous, but ν or π would also be anomalous   19]., a cross-stroke with a thickening at its left hand end level with the top of the letters   Of τ only the top, of α only the tail   .[, a hook to right level with the top of the letters   20 ..[, an upright descending below the line, followed by four dispersed traces at different levels   21 .[, the upper part of a slightly convex upright

Fr. 11 1 ἠ]μιθέων.

2 (-)c]τάδιον.

3 I do not think that π, though marginally preserved, can possibly be read as κ, so that δρά]κοντας ἀπλάτο[υc might be considered (for which cf. Pind. *Pyth.* xii 9, Bacchyl. v 62).

5 I can find no evidence for cιδήρεοc feminine. A figure sometimes found in the surroundings referred to in the note on l. 11, Atalanta, might perhaps be so qualified.

7 ὑφ᾽ ἅρμαcι cf. Pind. fr. 234 ὑφ᾽ ἅρμαcιν ἵπποc, *Isth.* v 5 schol.

8 (ἐ)ν]ικάcαν τρέχο[ντες.

9 A word beginning (as shown by the *trema*) with ιο followed by two letters and οc has a good chance of being Ἰόλαοc. But though λα (as written in l. 11) may be accommodated, I am bound to say that α would have to be supposed very anomalously formed. The internal argument for Iolaus l. 11 n.

Not prima facie ἀρήϊοc.

10 ἐπιβάντα is a natural guess, but I do not think reconcilable with such traces as remain.

11 Π]ηλεὺ[c] δὲ παλα- the exact form of words is not ascertainable, but I suppose there is not much doubt that there is a reference to Peleus as a wrestler. The most notable occasion on which he competed was the ἆθλα ἐπὶ Πελίαι (Apollod. *Bibl.* iii 9, 2, 4 seq., 13, 3, 1; Paus. v 17, 10; Hygin. 273), and at these Iolaus also competed (with a *quadriga*), at least according to Pausanias (l.c., description of the chest of Cypselus) and Hyginus (l.c.). Other details compatible with the hypothesis that these games are referred to may be found in ll. 1, 2, 7, 8, 12. But there are many others of which I cannot see the relevance to such a context, most strikingly of all ll. 17 seq.

12 κ]ῦδος ὑπέρτερον. If this refers to a victory in the games, it is to be noted that according to Apollodorus (l.c.) Peleus was defeated by Atalanta and according to Pausanias (l.c.) fought with Jason on equal terms. Only Hyginus (l.c.) makes him victorious.

13]αμεν, infinitive, οὐ δυν[α- a reasonable articulation. In l. 6 γαμέν also looks to me the likeliest interpretation.

17 seq. Chrysaor plays no part in legend except as father of Geryones. Geryones is an important figure in the Herakles story. Herakles was present (presided?, Pausanias (l.c.), competed, Hyginus (l.c.)) at the funeral games of Pelias. (It is possible that his name is to be recognized in l. 6 above.) Except for the fact that Stesichorus wrote an Ἆθλα ἐπὶ Πελίαι and a Γηρυονηίс in each of which Heracles appears, there is no connexion that I know of between the two stories.

Fr. 12

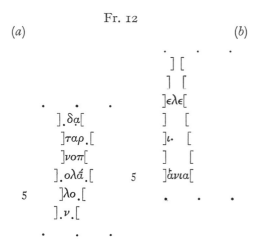

Fr. 12 The cross-fibres seem to run from (a) to (b), but there is nothing to show the distance between them

(a) 1]., I think α, but λ not ruled out   2 .[, a dot well below the line   4]., the extreme right-hand end of a cross-stroke touching the top of ο   .[, perhaps the top of the left-hand stroke of *ν*, but too damaged to verify   5 .[, I think *ν*, but *τ* may be possible   6]., the lower end of a stroke descending from left   .[, the upper end of a stroke descending to right

(*b*) 5 Over *α*[an accent, I think the left-hand end of a 'circumflex'

Fr. 13

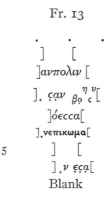

```
        ·     ·      ·
        ]     [
      ]αυπολιν [
      ].  ϛαν  βο  η ν[
                   ϛ
      ]όϵϲϲα[
      ].νϵπικωμα[
5       ]     [
      ]. ν  ϵϛα[
            Blank
```

Fr. 13 2]., the right-hand arc of a small circle, immediately followed by an upright with a projection to left at the top; does not much resemble the hand of the text   4 *marg.*]., looks like *ω* with a tail depending from the top of the right-hand stroke   6]., the right-hand base angle of *o* or *ω*?

Fr. 13 6 This line looks a little smaller and slighter than the three of the text above and might be an addition made in the lower margin.

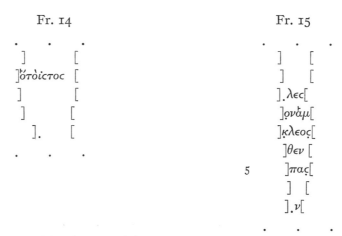

Fr. 14   Fr. 15

```
    ·     ·      ·                ·     ·      ·
    ]          [                 ]          [
  ]ότòιϲτοϲ [                    ]          [
    ]          [                 ].λϵϲ[
    ]          [               ]ονὰμ[
    ].         [               ]κλϵοϲ[
    ·     ·      ·               ]θϵν [
                              5  ]παϲ[
                                 ]     [
                                 ].ν[
                                   ·     ·      ·
```

Fr. 15 Smaller writing than any of the rest

1]., the lower end of a stroke descending from left   2 *α* ex *o*, first hand   5 For ϛ[perhaps *o* 7]., the top of *ϵ*? Above and to right of *ν* the start of a stroke rising to right, perhaps relating to l. 6

Fr. 15 A possibility to be considered is that ll. 1–5 of these verses were written in the upper margin, having been omitted in their place in the column. At least, that might account for the relatively small size of the writing.

Fr. 16

.   .   .

].μ..θεω..[

]ǫκλεακευρυϲθενη.[

]υχεταᾱ̆ᾱϲθạ[

]   [

5   ]   [

].ποιϲαπα.[

]   [

]βαινε..[

]λλι   [

10   ]λλέεραϲτ[

      [

      [

]ουϲαθ[

.   .   .

Fr. 16 1]., the foot of a slightly forward-sloping stroke   After μ a trace off the line, followed by two hooks to right like the lower part of ϲ, between the second of which and θ a hook to left off the line   ..[, the feet of two uprights, probably ν   2 *marg.* .[, an upright with ink, partly blurred, to right of its foot, and a suspended letter, perhaps αⱽ   6]., the right-hand edge of a circle   .[, a dot level with the top of the letters   A dot below the tail of the second α may belong to a marginal note   8 ..[, a dot on the line, followed by a dot below the line

On the back, at the top, traces of two widely separated lines

Fr. 16 2 *marg.* Πρ]οκλέα κ(αὶ) Εὐρυϲθένη the founders of the Eurypontid and Agiad lines of Spartan kings.

3 ε]ὐχετάαϲθα[ι hitherto not found in lyric, but only in epic, verse. I do not understand the marking of the second α as long. I suppose it is by analogy with active forms in -αᾶν.

10]λλέʼ, e.g. περικαλλέ(α)?

Fr. 17

```
              ·    ·
        ·              ·
        ]λε[
        ].επηρ[
        ].ουδε[
        ]περιδω[
  5     ]ρυϲεα[
        ]ϲοχετο . .[
        ]χθών·    [
        ].ελεφαν.[
          ].ϲ΄.[
 10     ]λμ᾿..[
             ᾿ι
        ].οϲο .[
        ].τει[
        ].νε[
        ]ργα[
 15       ].ε.[
          ·    ·    ·
```

Fr. 17 1 ϛ anomalous and more like θ, but not the θ of this hand   2]., the foot of an upright   3]., an upright   6 ..[, the lower part of an upright descending below the line, followed at an interval by a short flat stroke on the line   8]., a dot level with the top of the letters .[, traces compatible with the top of τ, but not verifiable   9]., a dot about mid-letter   .[, the lower part of an upright   10 Of]λ only the lower part of the right-hand stroke   After μ either α or ο, followed by a trace on the line   11]., the ends of divergent strokes, as of χ?   .[, the upper end of a stroke descending to right   12]., two vertically related dots opposite the left-hand end of τ   13]., the right-hand angle of ω?   15 .[, a speck some way from ϛ, not quite level with the top of the letters

On the back, at the top of the fragment, the remains of three lines].[].[
```
                                                                ]υγα[
                                                                ]τον[
```

Fr. 17 4 seq. Ἐϲ]περίδω[ν and χ]ρύϲεα (μᾶλα) are obvious possibilities.

Fr. 18

```
    ·    ·    ·
      ]..[
     ]βϱ.[
     ]εξ.[
     ].εῖ[
5    ]νι.[
     ] εξ[
     ]πα[
     ]φυ[
     ]μᾶ[
10   ]ῖο.[
    ·    ·    ·
```

Fr. 19

```
    ·    ·    ·
     ].εα.[
     ]..εκ[
     ]   [
     ]κπρ[
5    ]αλλὲ[
     ]   [
       ·    ·
```

Fr. 18 1 Traces compatible with the top of γ (or τ) and the apex of a triangular letter   2 .[, a trace on the line   3 .[, the left-hand side of a small circle at the level of the top of the letters; υ not suggested   4]., confused ink against ε at about the middle   5 .[, ο or less probably ϲ   6 Above ε a thick dot   10 .[, a dot level with the top of the letters

Fr. 19 1]., the right-hand end of a cross-stroke touching ε below the top   Between ε and α a high dot; perhaps part of a letter in the previous line   .[, the start of a stroke rising to right?   2].., the loop of ρ or possibly the right-hand side of ο, followed by a convex upright   Of κ[only the central lower part

Fr. 20

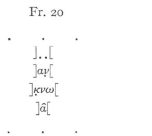

```
    ·    ·    ·
      ]..[
     ]αν[
     ]κνω[
     ]ᾶ[
    ·    ·    ·
```

Fr. 21

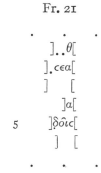

```
    ·    ·    ·
     ]..θ[
     ].ϲεα[
     ]   [
       ]α[
5    ]δοῖϲ[
     ]   [
       ·    ·    ·
```

Fr. 20 1 Prima facie]λλ[, but]α and ν[do not appear to be ruled out   2 Over α a 'long' or a rough breathing?   3 Of]κ only the ends of the upper and lower arms

Fr. 21 1].., perhaps the turn-up οι ε or the like, followed by the lower part of ϲ (or less probably ε)   2]., a short descending stroke against the upper part of ϲ   5 Of]δ only the bottom right-hand angle; φ perhaps not ruled out

Fr. 22

```
        .        .
       ]..[
      ]αιοι.[
      ]ιν̂ι.[
      ]  [
5     ].ον[
      ]..[
     .       .       .
```

Fr. 23

```
      .        .
     ].[
     ].α̂[
     ]ε.[
     .      .      .
```

Fr. 23 2]., perhaps the edge of the loop and elements of the stalk of φ, or ρ may be possible 3 .[, the foot of an upright, followed by a short arc from the lower left-hand side of a circle; perhaps π, or separate letters

Fr. 22 1 The lower right-hand arc of a circle, followed by the lower part of a stroke rising to right from below the line   2 .[, ο or perhaps ϲ   3 ν seems to have been made out of λ *currente calamo*   .[, a triangular letter, I think δ likeliest   5]., the extreme end of a stroke below the left-hand side of ο   6 The upper part of a stroke sloping gradually to right, followed by the tip of a stroke well above the level of the top of the letters

Fr. 24

```
      .       .       .
     ].[
     ].ηνα[
     ]να..[
     ]  [
     .      .      .
```

Fr. 25

```
      .        .        .
      ].γα[
      ].νο[
      ]κ.[
      .       .       .
```

Fr. 25 1]., I think λ likelier than α   2]., a trace of a stroke from left touching the middle of the left-hand upright of ν   3 .[, apparently the top and a trace of the lower left-hand side of a circle

Fr. 24 1 A horizontal stroke on the line 2]., the right-hand end of a cross-stroke touching η at the left-hand end of its cross-stroke Of α[only the loop   3 ..[, the right-hand stroke of a triangular letter, followed by the top of a stroke descending to right

Fr. 26

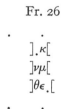

```
      .       .
     ].κ[
     ]νμ[
     ]θε.[
     .        .
```

Fr. 26 1]., the foot of an upright   3 .[, the left-hand arc of a circle

Fr. 27

(*a*)

```
        .   .      .
      ].νο.[
      ]μαχαιγιγαντες [
      ]μεναρήονεϲαλκα[
      ].[.]ταγενέ..[      (b)
  5   ]τωννὸὸν [
      ]υμφοραῖϲ[              .    .    .
      ]ν︮ε̈ρ︦ω̈[        ]εν  [
      ].υϲω[               ].ννεοικ[
                          ].οντε[
        .    .    .       ].ρόδε[
                      10  ]λυκεϲ.[
                          ]αεξὸμ[
                          ]αϲτοϲ[
                          ]ωϲδαῦ   [
                                 λ[
                          ]ἀγερώχοι· ᾳ[
                      15  ]οκρατηϲθᾳν[
                          ].ν[
                          .    .    .
```

Fr. 27 There is no external evidence to show the distance between (*a*) and (*b*).

1]., on the line a speck and at some distance to right the end of a stroke descending from left; *a* possible .[, the lower part of an upright descending below the line   2 Of]μ only the end of the right-hand stroke   4].[, the lower end of a stroke descending below the line   *a* ex *o*?   ..[, perhaps the tops of ϲθ   7 Above ω a dot perhaps indicating a v.l.   ]., on a single fibre the upper end of a stroke descending to right   Of ν only the top left-hand angle and the tip of the right-hand upright   8 (*a*)]., a dot slightly higher than mid-letter with the lower part of a stroke descending from left below it   (*b*)]., a speck on the line   9]., the right-hand end of a stroke level with the top of the letters; perhaps ε   10 Of]λ only the lower part of the right-hand stroke   .[, γ or π   12]α anomalous; perhaps made out of *o*

Fr. 27 2 A compound of -μάχηϲ seems as likely as μάχᾱι.

3 The accent indicates ἀρήονεϲ, precluding ἄρηον ἐϲ. Perhaps, therefore, ἀλκά[ν is implied.

4 γενέϲθ[αι.

5 I cannot guess what is meant by the accentuation. It would be appropriate to a compound word like νουνεχής, but to nothing that could be expected in lyric verses.

6 ϲ]υμφοραῖϲ[.

14 ἀγερώχοι laudatory, of persons (Alcman and) Bacchylides, of things Pindar.

15 -]οκρατὴϲ θαν[ατ-?

Fr. 28

·   ·   ·

]θ̣ε.[

αγαν.[
εικατα.[

]ραινωνι:[

]·ας̣φρενας[

]·ν   [

5   .^]ματα̣[

]   [

·   ·   ·

Fr. 28 1 Below θ the right-hand end of a curved stroke, perhaps a 'hyphen'   After ε a dot on the line followed by the extreme lower end of a stroke descending from left; perhaps two letters   *marg.* 1 .[, perhaps the lower part of ζ, followed by the foot of an upright   2 .[, a horizontal stroke level with the top of the letters, followed by what most resembles υ   3 *marg.*]., perhaps the right-hand edge of β   4]., indeterminate traces, perhaps of the right-hand arc of a circle

Fr. 29

·   ·

]νεω[

]βροτ̣[

] ιδεκ[

]κε κ̣[

] [

·   ·   ·

Fr. 30

·   ·

]·α[

]θε.[

]μεν[

]πὲν.[

5   ]ὸ̣χ[

·   ·

Fr. 30 1]., a median dot, followed by a dot on the line   Of α[only the loop   2 Of]θ only the middle of the right-hand side   .[, the upper left-hand arc of a small circle just above mid-letter, followed by a dot on the line   4 .[, the left-hand base angle of a triangle; δ suggested

Fr. 31

].ε[
]..μ.[
]..ιτη[
]ιζο[]ι.[
5   ]παν.[
]τωϲγ[
].[]λλα[

Fr. 31 The upper part rubbed

1]., the foot of a stroke hooked to right, at about mid-letter; ? an inserted letter   2 seq. In the left-hand margin the ends of three lines of small writing   2 Before μ the first letter of the line appears to be υ, represented by the left-hand end of the cross-stroke and the foot of the stalk   3 Besides ιτη a number of other combinations might be proposed, some more attractive as decipherments but not acceptable as elements of words   4 .[, the start of a stroke rising to right with a projection to right at its upper end   5 .[, the foot of an upright hooked to right or the left-hand side of the back of a loop?   6 seq. In the interlinear space between ω and]λ a heavy dot   7].[, a cross-stroke slightly above the top of the letters

Fr. 32

].[
].φι[
]αντ[
].[

Fr. 32 1 On the line a hook to right   2]., on the line the lower end of a stroke descending from left   3 Of]α only the tip and lower end of the right-hand stroke

Fr. 33

·   ·   ·

].[

].οτοι.[

]αρ επ[

]ἠϲ   [

·π·

5   ].οϲμό[

].[

·   ·   ·

Frr. 33–34 appear to come from the same column.

Fr. 33 1 On the line a short arc of the base of a circle   2]., the right-hand end of a loop, about mid-letter; ρ possible   .[, the left-hand arc of a circle; ϲ possible   3 *marg.* .[, the lower end of a slightly forward-sloping stroke   5]., the overhang of ϲ or the like?

Fr. 33 2 β]ροτοιϲ[possible.

The two parts of the marginal addition are apparently in different hands. The natural inference is that Ἀρι( ) is not the authority for ἐπ-.

Fr. 34

·   ·   ·

]ναρ.[

]δολοπ[

]φἀθ' ὠ[

].[[ι]]τεραϲ.[

5   ].νμελεων.[

]πικρατεϙ.[

].νουχοϲ.[

]νγαρνιν αν[

].νατοπ[.]τν[

10   ]αϲκορυφ[

].θεω[

].θανατα[

].νοι[.]α[

]νμ[

·   ·   ·

Fr. 34 1 .[, π acceptable; γ followed by a dot on the line not ruled out   3 Over the left-hand side of φ the right-hand end of a horizontal stroke   4]., the lower right-hand arc of a circle

with a tail hanging from its upper end; *o* or *ω*?   .[, a dot level with the top of the letters   5].,
the bottom right-hand angle of *o* or *ω* suggested   .[, a short arc of the left-hand side of a circle on
the line   6 Of *ω* only the left-hand and the top of the right-hand stroke   .[, a more or less
horizontal stroke level with the top of the letters, followed by another at the same level; *c*.[appears
possible   7]., a short nearly horizontal stroke, with a dot below its left-hand end, level with the
top of the letters   .[, the upper part of an upright   8 Of *α* only the lower part of the right-hand
stroke   9]., two dots side by side on the line; *η* acceptable   10 Of *φ* only the left-hand
loop, but not *δ*   11]., the lower end of a stroke descending from left   12]., the same
13]., a dot level with the top of the letters and a dot below it on the line

Fr. 34 2 δολοπ[λόκ- a fairly likely guess among the various possibilities.

6 ἐ]πικρατέως as at Stesich. fr. 40, 24 (but otherwise an epic word, Hom. *Il.*, Hesiod) looks likely.
Not -έων.

7 I cannot interpret the traces before *ν*. I should guess the articulation to be].*ν* οὐχ ὅσι[-. If
]εν- is a possible reading (which I cannot deny), for τεμενοῦχος see Pfeiffer on [Callim.] fr. 813. ἐ]ϋνοῦ-
χος, first, I suppose, in Hippon. fr. 35, 3, cannot be made out of the ink.

9 -]ήνατο π[ο]τν[ι-?

10 -]ας κορυφ[ας.

12 ἀθανατα[(-).

Fr. 35

·   ·   ·

]   [

]κεν [

·   ·   ·

Frr. 35–37 appear to come from the same column

Fr. 36

·   ·   ·

].[

].ιδαι.[

]...ω.[

]..τοι[

5   ].είρυ.[

]γναν[

'].εναν[

]ἴκ.[

·   ·   ·

Fr. 36 1 The lower end of a stroke descending below the line   2]., a slightly dipping cross-
stroke touching the top of *ι* with a speck below its left-hand end; perhaps *γ* or *τ*   .[, a dot below the
line   3]..., a dot just below the line, followed by a dot on the line, and this by the lower end of
a stroke descending from left suggesting *κ*   .[, a dot below the line. I am far from sure that what

I have represented as ω.[should not be, less obviously but more correctly, interpreted as ον[4].., a thick dot just off the line, followed by the lower end of a stroke descending from left, e.g. α   5]., the lower end of a stroke descending from left   .[, the left-hand arc of a circle well off the line 6]γ rather anomalous   7]., the right-hand end of a cross-stroke level with the top of the letters 8 ˫ is incomplete to left, but I think likelier than ¯   Of κ only the tips of the upright and upper branch   .[, I think the left-hand part of a short over a lost letter, not part of a letter

Fr. 37

.   .

].ς..[
].τονη[
]αλοχ[

.   .

Fr. 37 1]., the foot of an upright   ..[, the lower part of a slightly forward-sloping stroke, followed by the lower left-hand side of a small circle or loop; possibly a single letter, e.g. η or π, but I think the spacing suggests rather τ.[2]., a short arc from the top right-hand side of a circle

Fr. 38

.   .

].ω[
]δοχυ[
]cοκὰρ[
].διν.[

.   .

Fr. 38 There is a 'joint' visible at the bottom right-hand corner

1]., the lower part of an upright, some way from ω   4]., the overhang of c?   .[, the top of a circle

Fr. 39

.   .

].ρ[
].κεα[
]δεν [

.   .

Fr. 39 1]., a cross-stroke touching ρ below the top   2]., the right-hand side of ω acceptable

Fr. 40

.   .

]   [

]νατων   [
]τρᾰ̈πέτα[
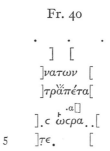
].c ὡcρα..[
5   ]τε.   [

Fr. 40 On the back remains of a line of writing parallel to the height of the roll.

4]., I think ο, but cannot quite rule out ω Above this verse a horizontal stroke extending at one level as far as]τ, l. 3, and, after a short rise, at another level as far as α; perhaps intended for a 'hyphen'   ..[, λ followed by a dot level with the top of the letters looks likely, but ν[not to be ruled out   5 After ε prima facie ο, but possibly a large c

Fr. 40 3 The signs seem to imply a word containing -τραπέτᾰ(ι) or alternatively -τράπετᾰ(ι), but I have not guessed what it is.

Fr. 41

```
      ]δετ[
     ].κια·[
     ].ναι[
     ]λέγει[
5    ]οκαι[
```

Fr. 42

```
      ].υππ[
     ].αυχ[
     ]ωϲ [
     ]κυκλ[
5    ]         [
     ]φίκον [
     ]αϲεπητ[
     ].υνέ[
     ]αϲ [
10   ]ϲιϲ [
```

Fr. 41 2]., the lower part of a stroke descending from left   The stop is rather anomalous; perhaps it represents an interlinear letter   3]., the lower end of a stroke from left   4 Of]λ only the tail

Fr. 41 4 The accent might be taken to imply λέγεν, but though ι is close to the edge, ν looks unacceptable.

Fr. 42 1]., on the line the lower right-hand arc of a circle   2]., the middle of the right-hand side of a circle, close to α   7 Of τ[only the left-hand end of the cross-stroke against the right-hand angle of η   8]., the right-hand end of a cross-stroke slightly below the top of the letters   9 Of]α only the end of the tail

Fr. 43

```
     ]ωκ[
     ]ονεϲ·α.[
     ]ῶντεπο[
```

Fr. 43 2 .[, the left-hand end of a slightly dipping cross-stroke, as of τ or υ

Fr. 44

Col. i   Col. ii

```
]ν       ].αι.[[.]][
]        πρᾶ.[
```

Fr. 44 There is a 'joint' down the middle
1 Before α the foot of an upright   After ι a cross-stroke with a dot about mid-letter below its left-hand end and touching with its right-hand end the top of a heavily cancelled upright; apparently π made into γ[[ι]]. The apparent dot above the cancelled upright is not in the same ink, and perhaps not ink at all   2 .[, the lower part of an upright

Fr. 45

Col. i   Col. ii

```
              ·        ·       ·
                    ]αι[
                    ] χα[
            ]ʲ   εξ[
            ]     ν.[
    ]ε       α.[              5
    ]υ°
    ]υ       ερ[
    ]        γὴ[
            ]να[
    ]        κε[
              ·        ·       ·
```

Fr. 45 Col. ii 1 ι looks like an insertion, though apparently by the original hand   4 .[, perhaps the hook of the left-hand end of the cross-stroke of υ   5 .[, the edge of the lower part of an upright   6 For ρ[I cannot rule out λ

Fr. 46   Fr. 47

```
    ·        ·                  ·        ·
]ντ..[                      ]ας [
]ιδεβρ.[                    ]ς..[
].ν   [                       ·        ·
].   [
  ·     ·     ·
```

Fr. 47 1 Of]α only the extreme end of the tail, touching ς   2 Of]ε only the top   ..[, a stroke starting above the top of the letters and descending to right to mid-letter, e.g. λ, followed by a dot opposite its lower end

Fr. 46 1 ..[, a speck on the line, followed by a horizontal stroke on the line   2 .[, the lower left-hand arc of a circle   3]., the right-hand base angle of ο or ω

Fr. 48

```
    ·        ·       ·
]ους  [
]ληιτο.[
]αν  [
].[
  ·     ·     ·
```

Fr. 48 There appears to be a 'joint' at the right-hand edge.
2 .[, the middle part of an upright

Fr. 49

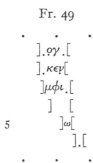

```
        ·       ·     ·
      ].ο̩γ.[
      ].κεγ̣[
      ]μφι.[
      ]     [
5     ]ω[
          ].[
          ·       ·     ·
```

Fr. 49 There is a 'joint' not far from the right-hand edge.

1]., the turn-up of a stroke from left, e.g. μ   .[, a short upright against the right-hand end of the bar of γ   2]., a stroke descending from left to the middle of κ; λ suggested   3 .[, γ or the left-hand part of π   5 Smaller than ll. 1–3

Fr. 50

```
        ·     ·    ·
      ]. . .[
      ]ε̣ρδέα[
      ]οισα[
      ]νο̣[
        ·     ·    ·
```

Fr. 51

```
        ·     ·    ·
      ]οϲτιϲα̣[
      ]καϲτο[
      ]μονε[
      ]οιϲψ.[
5     ]ιϲθε[
      ]θλο[
        ·     ·
```

Fr. 50 1]. ., a horizontal stroke at mid-letter, perhaps ε, followed by the lower part of a stroke rising to right   .[, a trace on the line 2 Of]ε only the tip of the overhang and the end of the cross-stroke; above ερ a horizontal stroke with a small sign, r, at its right-hand end I am not sure that what I have rendered as an 'acute' on ε is not an interlinear letter; there is more ink than is accounted for   For ω[I cannot rule out δ

Fr. 51 4 .[, perhaps the lower left-hand part of a circle or loop, e.g. α[, but very faint

Fr. 52

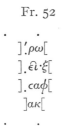

```
        ·     ·    ·
      ]΄.ρω[
      ].ε̣ι·ξ[
      ].ϲαφ[
      ]ακ[
        ·     ·
```

Fr. 52 1]., the right-hand base angle of ο or ω as of τ   3]., the right-hand base angle of ο or ω that υ, though not made as usual, is not preferable   2]., the right-hand part of a cross-stroke, φ[is rather high in the line. I am not sure

Fr. 53   Fr. 54

```
         .    .   .                    .    .   .
        ].[                           ]εφ[
        ]φο[                          ]εα[
        ]αήτα[                        ]δε.[
        ]καιο[                        ]ρε.[
    5   ]ταcυ[
                                       .    .   .
         .    .   .
```

Fr. 54 3 .[, c suggested, but only the left-hand part remains   4 .[, a dot level with the top of the letters

Fr. 53 1 A hook to right on the line 4 ạ made out ο   Over ọ what looks like a 'grave', but uncommonly low

2736. CHORAL LYRIC (?PINDAR)

Of the three principal composers of choral lyric, to which category of verse the following tatters seem plainly to belong, it is Pindar, not Simonides or Bacchylides, to whom it is reasonable to ascribe them, though the hypothesis rests on no more than the use of the form γλεφάρωι (not βλεφάρωι) at fr. 2 (*b*) 17. Identification of the author is of no particular advantage. Apart from the three mentions of Heracles and the treatment at some length of the sack of Oechalia I can form no coherent idea about the contents of the piece. It may be suspected that a good deal is lost of the right-hand side of each column.

Of the metrical constitution likewise I can give no account. The coronis would be expected to mark the division between pericopae, the paragraphus the internal division between strophes. But there is no obvious metrical correspondence between the verses above and below the coronis in Fr. 1 ii and those above and below the coronis in Fr. 2 (*a*). The only correspondence I see in the whole of the evidence is that of the short verses Fr. 1 ii 19 and Fr. 2 (*a*) 6, below the first of which is a paragraphus, below the second a paragraphus cum coronide. But again there is no correspondence in the verses above and below each of these. A further anomaly, if Fr. 2 (*a*) starts at the top of a column, is that the paragraphus divides the verses between the first coronis and the second into two unequal blocks of sixteen and eleven.

The text is written in a medium-sized bookhand of a common type, comparable, for instance, with **7,** ascribed to the third century. There are a few lection signs some of which may be by a different pen. The papyrus is in an exceptionally bad state of preservation. What makes it difficult to handle is the looseness of the surface, and in many places frayed out or floating fibres make decipherment precarious through displacement of the ink.

Fr. 1

Col. i Nothing preserved   Col. ii
but]ν· opposite ii 15

$$\cdot \qquad \cdot \qquad \cdot$$

```
          ].ϲι[].[
          ]οντω[
     ὅ   τ...[]οντα.[
     ⊕   ὁρμανδο.[
  5       απω[.]α.[.
          ὀκνῳ[.]πα.αλ[
          οψινο.ρ.[
          ωνυ[.].ατον[
          ..[  ]μενοϲπολ[].[
 10       μο..[ ].[].νειϲαϊδανε[
     [  .]δα...ροτ᾿αφρωνπο[
     [  ] ειδωϲ[.].ένητονκαι[
     [  ].ανατοϲκαθελωνπα[
     [  .]..μενοιναν·καιε.[
 15  [  ].[].ἐιμε[..]εντιδοκεο[
          πολιναϲ[.]κυλοτοξωνε[
          ναϲαρξ[.]ναοιδαϲπρω[
          ηρακλ[..]καιτανλιπαρο[
          α.[..]βαν
 20       ξανθανχρυϲοπεδ[...]οι[
          δωϲϊκετοεϲοιχα[
          χινιονχαλκαϲπι[
          νεαμεντελ[
          χ.ννυκταϲτεα[
```

Fr. 1 To left of ll. 2–8 of Col. ii is a blank area of papyrus, of a width much greater than the usual space between columns, which is more or less what is seen to left of ii 17.

Col. ii has broken in two along the line of a 'joint', and as a result of subsequent warping the parts cannot now be laid so that all the verses run continuously at the same time.

Col. ii 1]., level with the top of the letters, two dots side by side on a single fibre   ϲ damaged, but ε apparently less likely   3 ...[, dispersed traces; the count is uncertain   .[, the left-hand part of a cross-stroke, as of τ, with a trace below, prima facie ξ likely   4 Though the alignment of ὁ is not quite correct, there was no letter before it   .[, a speck on the line   5 .[, a dot near the line, perhaps on the underlayer; above the following letter interlinear ink   6 Of ῳ[only the top of the left-hand stroke   Between α and α specks compatible with the stalk of ρ but not suggesting it   7 Between ο and ρ perhaps the right-hand loop of φ   .[, the lower part of an upright   8]., the right-hand end of a cross-stroke level with the top of the letters   9 ..[, the lower end of a stroke descending below the line, followed by a cross-stroke, level with the top of the letters, having a dot below its left-hand end   10 Of ρ only the base   ρ is followed by a hook to right on the line, and this by a forward-sloping stroke   ].[, the foot of an upright   ]., the right-hand arc of a small circle; ο or ρ suggested   11 Between α and ρ apparently the extreme top and bottom of an upright, followed by the lower end of a faint stroke curving down from left and this by a dot on the line and the top of a stroke which appears to split at the lower end   12]., γ or the right-hand part of τ   13]., a short horizontal stroke on a single fibre   14].., specks, on right of which a headless upright descending well below the line   .[, γ or the left-hand angle of π   15].[, the tip of an upright, faint   ]., the upper part of an upright   17 Between c and π above the line the upper right-hand arc of a small circle, followed by a short horizontal stroke   18]κ, only the extreme ends of the arms, but not χ   Of ρ[, only the lower left-hand arc   19 .[, prima facie μ or ν, but λ may not be ruled out   21 Above ω traces   22 Of ι[only the thickened tip   24 Between χ and ν there is now no ink, but in an earlier transcript I find χων

Fr. 1 Col. ii 3 The coronis implies a paragraphus under this line, but I cannot tell whether or not one was written.

4 The accent presents a problem I cannot solve. As appears from Bacchyl. xvi 13–end the mention of the river Λυκόρμας would not be out of place in the context implied by the proper names found in the lower part of this and in the next fragment. But κόρ- was not written and Λυκ-όρ- is an unacceptable division.

7 ὄψιν, perhaps followed by ὀφρυ[.

8 ὕ[c]τατον suggested.

10 If εἰς, Ἀΐδα νε[- prima facie preferable to Ἀΐδαν ε[, since Pindar has no example of εἰς Ἀΐδαν[1] but says εἰς Ἀΐδα cταθμόν Ol. x 92, εἰς Ἀΐδα δόμον Pyth. iii 11. -ον, but not δόμον, may have preceded in this verse.

12 [ἀ]γένητον.

13 θάνατος καθελών. Cf. Pind. Ol. ix 60 μὴ καθέλοι μιν αἰών. Harpocr. Lex. i 165 καθελών· Δημοσθένης ἐν τῶι κατ᾽ Ἀριστοκράτους . . . ἀντὶ τοῦ ἀνελών . . . ὡς καὶ Cτησίχορος ἐν Ἰλίου πέρςιδι καὶ Cοφοκλῆς ἐν Εὐμήλωι.

14 Presumably μενοινᾶν infinitive. The present participle three times in Pindar; no example in Simonides or Bacchylides. The noun μενοινή Hellenistic.

15 {ε}ἱμε[ρό]εντι (or -[ρό]εν τι)?

16 In view of the references below it is a reasonable guess that in ἀγκυλοτόξων there is allusion to the family of Eurytus, lord of Oechalia, all famous archers.

17 ἄρξ[ο]ν ἀοιδᾶς, addressed to the Muse? At any rate the narration of Heracles' sack of Oechalia seems to begin here.

19 ἀμ[οι]βαν seems likeliest, though an explanation of its situation between ταν λιπαρο[- and ξανθαν is not easy to think of. Perhaps the postulation of a full-stop after it is sufficient. (It may prevent trouble, if I say that Δαϊ|αν[ει]ραν is out of the question.)

20 χρυσοπέδιλος again in choral lyric at **2621** fr. i ii 32.

21 seq. ἵκετ᾽ ἐς Οἰχα[λίαν..... Τρα]χίνιον I take the general sense to be, that Heracles left Trachis (where Ceyx was harbouring him) and came to Oechalia, the consequences of his attack on which are recognizable in Fr. 2 (a) 7 seqq.

21 The *scriptio plena* is unexpected in a manuscript of this date and I do not see any particular advantage gained from its use. ἵκετες, though it is theoretically ambiguous, does not seem likely to be misunderstood.

22 Some form of χάλκαςπις probable.

---

[1] Nor has any other lyric poet. For Ἀΐδα δόμος and analogous expressions preceded by εἰς, ἐν cf. Sappho fr. 55, 3, Alcaeus 48, 15; 296 (a) 5, Aristot. 842, 14 PMG.

Fr. 2

(*a*)

```
           .    .    .       .
   ...].[]ονο.το[[ι]]ν.λι[ ].  .[
   ...]αντιμαχοιτ[.]ξω[   ]ν[
   αμννομεν.διοϲδ.κ.[
   ϲφαραγουυιοϲμαρτυριαιϲ.[
5  πολεμοντερψιμβροτον[
   ⌜εθηκεν            [
   κλυτιον τ'αδειμ[.]ντονμ[
   ϲιδαϊξαϲμ..αθυμουτ[
   καν·καιευπλοκαμονπ[
10 γνητωυ[.]ανοντων[
   νεκυωνδιαρηϊφ[.]τωυ[
      ].[ ]ιολε[.]ανχαιρ.[
          ]αδ.[
          .    .    .
```

Fr. 2 (*a*) Apparently the top of a column; no doubt above fr. 2 (*b*), but I cannot determine at what interval.

1].[, the lower part of a forward sloping stroke   Between *o* and *τ* the lower part of an upright on a single fibre   After *ν* an upright, before λ the lower end of a stroke descending from left 1 seq. The two separated upright strokes at the end of l. 1 and the bottom right-hand angle of *ν* at the end of l. 2 certainly belong to this corner, but I am not sure whether I have got them opposite the right lines   3 Of *ν* only the extreme lower end of the stalk   Between *ν* and δ elements of an upright, nearer δ   Between δ and κ a dot on a single fibre   .[, a triangular letter; perhaps λ likeliest   4 .[, the foot of an upright   7 ον Of ο only the top, of *ν* the foot of the left-hand upright   Apparently ο[[ν]]μ[intended   8 Of ξ only the right-hand end of the base   10 Of ω only the right-hand stroke   12 Of ε[only the right-hand ends of the overhang and the cross-stroke   Of]α only the underside of the loop and the lower end of the right-hand stroke   .[, an upright close to the break

Fr. 2 (*a*), (*b*) I cannot follow the cross-fibres from fr. 1, but I do not think it can be doubted that fr. 2 represents the next column.

(*a*) 2 ἀντίμαχοϲ was hitherto unknown to verse and only late attested even in prose. Although the letters can be articulated so as to avoid it, it seems certain that ἀντίμαχοι τόξω[must be recognized.

3 I suppose ἀμυνόμεν[ο]ι, but οι must have been crushed; and ι is so much damaged that I cannot rule out ϲ.

3 seq. Διὸϲ ....[ἐρι|ϲφαράγου υἱόϲ, Heracles. Cf. Pind. fr. 6*a* (**d**), Bacchyl. v 20.

5 The only other instance of τερψίμβροτοϲ in lyric verse is at Bacchyl. xiii 72, where it is in the plural and what it qualifies is lost (presumably something like songs or dances). Otherwise it occurs only in hexameters (twice in the *Odyssey* and once in the Homeric hymn to Apollo) applied to the sun. I do not remember any passage in Greek where the notion expressed by 'delight of battle' appears.

7 Κλυτίοϲ—the accentuation prescribed by Herodian and attested in **2359** fr. 1 i 4—was the name of, among others, one of the four sons of Eurytus (**2481** fr. 5 (*b*) iii 29 seq.).

If I am not mistaken about the cancellation of ν, αδειμαντονμ[αχαν may have been converted into αδειμαντομ[αχαν. ἀδειμαντομάχας is not recorded, but has a parallel in form in ἀκαμαντομάχας (Pind. *Pyth.* iv 171, *pae.* xxii **f** 6), in meaning in ἀταρβομάχας (Bacchyl. xvi 28).

7 seq. -cι δαΐξας 'having killed' by such and such means?, along with such and such persons?

8 If I am right in recognizing an acute on the first ν, μεγαθύμου is indicated, though I cannot verify it. It is a rare word in lyric verse, occurring only once, Bacchyl. xiii 195.

9 εὐπλόκαμον the mention of brothers makes it reasonably sure that Iole is referred to. εὐπλόκαμος is not found in Pindar, but occurs twice in Bacchylides and as a variant in a quotation of Simonides. In this verse ἐΰ- might be expected; it was not written.

9 seq. κασι|γνήτων θανόντων their names in **2481** fr. 5 (*b*) iii 29 seq. (from schol. Soph. *Trach.* 266).

11 ἀρηϊφάτων ἀρηϊ-, ἀρεί- φατος hitherto only epic and dramatic.

12 Though the letters are susceptible of more than one other interpretation, it is reasonable in the context to see in them 'Ιολείαν, Iole, the daughter of Eurytus, 'Ιόλαν at Bacchylides xvi 27.

Fr. 2

(*b*)

```
              .    .    .      .

                    ].[
            ται. . λαμο[
            ρω. αφονο.[
            αναγκαιδοδ[
       5    φιτρυωνια[
            γυναικεστι[
            νηλησαιcα.[
              .ε..τα.ωcπ[         ].ξ[
             ]αιγαρτον.ολο[     ]παοι.[
      10    .].εραcιπλοκαμ[.].[.].οcτεβουλ[
             ]ωΐcθηκακονεξαλοcευρεια[
             ]νόιcεινκυπαριccοκομαν.[
            ']λχανινεπ[.']νωcεγυναικ[
             ]αντεccινωτυραννιαζευcκ[
      15      ].ανθρωποιcιμοιραν.[
              ]..ονθοαικὰρικαταφθιμ[
               ].τιcυνγλεφαρωιθὰ.[
               ].αμετεραν[..]ιλήθ.[
                ]ρὶτερπ.[
      20       ].ᾶνα.[
                ]ν[ ]..[

              .    .    .      .
```

Fr. 2 (*b*) 2 After ι the lower part of a slightly forward-sloping stroke   Before λ the right-hand stroke of α or λ   3 Between ω and α a dot on the line, nearer α   .[, the left-hand apex of μ or ν   4 Of δ only the tip of the right-hand stroke and the turn-up of the right-hand base-angle   Of δ[only the left-hand base-angle   7 Of ς only the right-hand end of the top and the left-hand side of the lower part   .[, the left-hand base-angle of ζ suggested, or possibly ξ; not prima facie δ   8 Before ε the upper end of a stroke rising from left   After ε the upper left-hand arc of a small circle, followed by the upper part of ε or ϲ   Between α and ω the lower part of a stroke descending from left   ]., the lower part of an upright descending below the line   9 Between ν and ο the top and lower end of a stroke descending to right   Of λ only the lower part of the left-hand and a speck from about the middle of the right-hand stroke; χ may be an alternative   .[, two traces on the line on a single fibre; δ perhaps acceptable   10]., three dots on a curve rising from left to right   ].[, elements of the lower part of an upright descending below the line   ]., the upper part of an upright   12 .[, an upright   13 αιϰ[, there is ink not accounted for between α and ι, namely, the top of an upright inserted between them, and ι itself is represented only by a couple of dots   14 τυ represented only by the lower parts of the stalks   ᾳ anomalous, the top of the right-hand stroke being too flat   αζ, over α the base of a circle resembling a 'short'   15]., the middle part of an upright   .[, an upright   16]., the tip and the lower part of a tall upright, followed by the foot of ε or ϲ   17]., the top of an upright   ιϲ have been retouched   .[, an upright with traces to its right   18]., three median dots together on a single fibre   ᾳ no longer verifiable   .[, elements of an upright   19 .[, the upper end of a slightly forward-sloping stroke   20 .[, γ or the left hand part of π

Fr. 2 (*b*) 4 seq. Ἀμ|φιτρυωνιά[δα(-).

7 νηλής as at Pind. *Pyth.* xi 22. νηλὲς αἶϲα cf. μοῖρ' ὀλοά Bacchyl. v 121.

9 Among other possibilities ἐπαοιδαί in some case to be remembered; three times in Pindar, not elsewhere in lyric verse.

10 ἐραϲιπλοκαμ- rare in lyric verse: Pind. *Pyth.* iv 136 (Ibyc. **303** PMG), not elsewhere.
-μ[ο]υ possible, not verifiable.

Διός τε βουλ[is a possibility suggested by the existence of many instances of this type of phrase: Pind. *Ol.* vi 46, *Isthm.* iii/iv 37 δαιμόνων βουλ-αῖϲιν, -αῖϲ, fr. 61, 4 τὰ θεῶν βουλεύματα; Bacchyl. ix 90 θεῶν βουλα[, xi 12 βουλαῖϲι θεῶν μακάρων; Stes. fr. 32 i 8 βουλαῖϲ Ἀθάναϲ; Ibyc. fr. 1 (*a*) 4 Ζηνὸϲ . . . βουλαῖϲ. But it cannot be verified and there are other choices.

11 seq. There is room for a letter before ὠΐϲθη.[1]

So far as I know, no form of οἴομαι is found in lyric verse, but I see no acceptable alternative to ὠΐϲθη (cf. *Od.* iv 453, xvi 475); 'fancied . . . would fetch up (ἀνοίϲειν) out of the wide sea'.

12 κυπαριϲϲόκομοϲ cited in schol. *Il.* xiii 132 as an example of the proparoxytone accentuation of compounds of κόμη, -κόμηϲ only here. Cf. ὀρέων κορυφὰϲ . . . δενδροκόμουϲ Aristoph. *Nub.* 279 seq. ὁ δενδροκόμηϲ Ἐρύμανθοϲ Rufin. *Anth. Pal.* v 18, 5.

12 seq. Presumably some natural feature is referred to, which may have its name attached. I cannot elicit either from the letters at the beginning of l. 13, in which (particularly if ἵν(α) 'where' is to be recognized) it should lie. There is no paroxytone word ending -λχη, -λχηϲ except κάλχη. I do not know whether the proper name Χάλκη is ever spelt Κάλχη (as Καλχ- and Χαλκ-ηδων are interchanged). In any case, there seems to be no room for more than one letter at the beginning of the line, for though in some MSS. the left-hand edge of the column moves leftwards as the column descends, in this, to judge by ll. 2–8, it remains vertical.

16 I suppose θοᾶι καρὶ καταφθιμ[εν-, not θοαί, καρὶ κ.

17 γλε-, not βλε-, regularly[2] in Pindar, βλε- in Bacchylides (five times including the compound ἰοβλ.) and apparently in Simonides (but only in a quotation).

---

[1] A single letter might represent an elided monosyllable, e.g. δέ, or the elided last syllable of a word not completed in the previous line, e.g. -δα, or a divided compound, e.g. ὑ|πω-. I mention this last possibility on account of the mysterious entry in Hesychius ὑποΐζεϲθαι· ὑπονοεῖν. If this is ὑπ-οΐζεϲθαι, it might have an aorist ὑπωΐϲθη (or have been deduced from it).

[2] Out of nine instances γλ- in six, γλ- with variant βλ- in two, βλ- only in compound ἑλικοβλ-, *Pyth.* iv 172.

19 Except for the doubtfully read name in IG xii 3 suppl. 1416, 1450 (Χαριτέρπης) and περιτερπής, with which Emathius is credited, no Greek word contains the collocation of letters ριτερπ. There is no theoretical objection to ἀρι- or ἐρι-τερπής, the second the more probable, since compounds with ἐρι- are a good deal commoner than those with ἀρι-, but neither is recorded.

Fr. 3

·   ·   ·
]ν[.]..[
]δοτοϲολβρ[
]οιδιμα᾽.[
·   ·   ·

Fr. 3 1]..[., traces on the line (? a flat stroke), followed by the foot of an upright and the start of a stroke rising to right. Perhaps three letters represented   3 .[, ν or possibly μ. Above the line, between α and this letter, what looks like a small o with a faint stroke rising out of its top and curving over to right

Fr. 3 2 Pindar has Διόϲδοτος twice, θεόϲδοτος twice, θεόδοτος once, Bacchylides θεόδοτος once. One of these seems to me the only recorded compound of -δοτος likely to have preceded ὄλβος. Cf. Pind. *Ol.* ii 36 θεόρτωι ϲὺν ὄλβωι (and more distantly *Nem.* viii 17, ix 45).

   3 ἀ]οιδιμαν[the evidence, as far as it goes, shows that ἀοίδιμος has only two terminations; Pind. *Ol.* xiv 3, Fr. 76.

2737. COMMENTARY ON A PLAY OF ARISTOPHANES

Parts of three, probably consecutive, columns of a ὑπόμνημα on a play, pretty certainly of Aristophanes, but of which I have found no clue to the identification. Of those *lemmata* of which enough remains for the metre to be recognizable, namely those in i 5 seqq., 19 seq(q.), 27 seqq., ii 18, ii 19 seqq., the sequence of metres is anapaestic, dactylic, trochaic, dactylic, trochaic, and there can be little doubt that Professor Fraenkel is right in seeing in them the anapaests, ode, epirrhema, antode, and antepirrhema of the parabasis of the comedy.

The text at the commentator's disposal appears to have been to some extent defective, i 11 seqq. The amount of learning displayed is about the average of the extant scholia. At i 26 a quotation is correctly assigned to its source, as it seems in contradiction of Aristarchus, Euphronius, and an authority referred to mysteriously as ὁ τὴν παραπλοκήν. In ii 10 seqq. a statement of Eratosthenes, if I have rightly interpreted it, produces a new piece of evidence about the assignment of choruses for comedies at the Lenaea. There is mention of a hitherto unknown play of Plato and the identification of a quotation of the first words of Alcman's first poem.

There is one certain error in the text, the omission of an essential word, in i 27. I do not see how to avoid the positing of corruption at i 21 seq.

The intended system of articulation appears to be: in the left-hand margin a *diple* at the beginning, a paragraphus at the end, of each *lemma*, internally a blank space before and after. But the intention has not been carried out with exactitude. For instance, there is no blank in i 15; the *diple* is misplaced at ii 34 seq.; in fr. 2 there are consecutive paragraphi (ll. 17–18, 20–21) without an intervening *diple*. There are besides blanks that seem to be without particular significance. There is a very slight projection of the lemma into the left-hand margin in some places in fr. 1 ii and fr. 2, but this, too, is erratic, as may be seen at the bottom of fr. i ii.

The text is written in a decent informal hand I suppose assignable to the late second century. A single or double comma-like 'filler' is used to keep the right-hand margin of the column even. The copyist has two *v*s, the commoner not different from his *κ* deprived of its lower arm, and a *τ* made by doubling back from the right-hand end of the cross-stroke (note i 25).

Fr. 1

<table>
<tr><td>Col. i</td><td>Col. ii</td></tr>
</table>

Col. i

.   .   .   .

```
            ]τοστουτ[
            ]τατονδ.[...]ον'[
        ].ααποδιοτιμουεφου[
        ]ονοιαριστοφανους.[
 5      ].λεις εδιδαχθησαντη-
        ]μηνϊζουσινοπωϲβα[]

        ].ηενλειψυδριαιπου[]
        ]ματοσαυθισαπαντλη[]
        ]παλαιονλουτριονα[
 10     ]ωτος μετατοπ[    ]
        ].φερεταιτολοιπον
        ]τιχουταχανουντο
        ].σαφεϲλογουτουεξηϲ„
        ]τιχωνσαφεσανην„
 15     ]πληρωμ[..]ο[ ]ϲτ.[

        ]..ληνογεν[    ]τ.[
        ]φηϲ[]λουτριο.[ ]. [

        ]εγουϲιτινεϲ α.[
        ]ροειρηται ενιππευσι κυ
 20     ]οσυποπτερυγωντοιονδε
        ]τομεναρισταρχειονδο„
        ]υνοτιτερπανδρουεστι-
        ]αρχηευφρονιοϲδεϲρτιεκ
        ]ων·ι[.·]νοϲμελωνοδετη-
 25     ]αραπλοκηνοτιεκτωναλ
        ]μανοϲεστιδεκτωνεισομη

        ]ονϋμνων αλλεχρηνχορο-
        ]δοντας[.].ονεπιληναι
        ]σκοπε[.]νε.[...]..[]εστιπ[]ι
 30     ]νειθ.[          ]εται
        ]ϲτων.[     ].[   ]ωνμα
        ].[          ]ωνειστον

                      ].τωνδε
                      ]ηναϊκον
```

Col. ii

.   .   .   .   .

```
        ]νειναιταθεα[
        ].κατοδεληναϊκ[
        ]ριωϲενδοξο[
        ]ιταχακαιδιατοε[
 5      ]μμαχ[....]ηδηαφ[
        ].α.[      ]νκαταθ[
        .[        ]αγματ[
        ϲομεν[    [ρυϲτ.[

        πολινε[      ]δηταδιο
 10     νυσια φ[ ]...ερατοϲ.ε
        νηϲπεριπλατωνοσοτι
        εωϲμεν[..]λοισεδιδουτας
        κωμωιδιασευδοκιμειδι
        αυτουδεπρωτονδιδαξας
 15     τουϲραβδουχουσκαιγενο„
        μενοϲτεταρτοσαπεωϲθη
        ]παλινειϲτουϲληναϊκους

        ]χρυσοκομαφιλομολπε αλ
        ]κμανοϲηαρχη ωϲδικαιον

 20     ]ευθεωϲκαταπαλα[.]εινεστι
        τουτ..[ ]υϲνεουϲδιδα

        ϲκαλο[ ]υτοβουλεται„
        λεγεινκ[ ]απαλαιεϲθαιτου
        .[ ].του.[ ]ϋποτων„
 25                 ]λων ευτ.
                    ]ωνταιαι.[
                    ]ιολι..[

        .[ ].ν.[
        ματτοντ.[

 30     τουβολουϲ[
        δοτι..ατ.[
        λεγονμαλ[
        εριωντη.[
        βραγμενηνδιαλελυμ[
 35     ειτανεναγμενηνπαλι[
        ]...νοϲεστιπαντωϲω[
```

Fr. 1

Col. i   Col. ii

.   .   .   .

                    μὲ]ν εἶναι τὰ θεα[

                    ].κα τὸ δὲ Ληναϊκ[

]τοςτουτ[   ]ρίως ἔνδοξο[

]τατονδ.[. . .]ον›   ]ι τάχα καὶ διὰ τὸ ε[

].α ἀπὸ Διοτίμου, ἐφ᾽ οὗ [5   cυ]μμαχ[. . . .]ηδη αφ[

πρῶτ]ον οἱ Ἀριστοφάνους› [   ].α.[   ]ν καταθ[

5   Δαιτ]αλεῖς ἐδιδάχθησαν. τὴν   .[   ]αγματ[

                ]μην ἴζουςιν ὅπως βα[-]

                         cομεν[   ]ροςτ.[

      ].η ἐν λειψυδρίαι που [ ]

]ματος αὖθις ἀμιιντλη[ ]   πόλιν ε[   ]δη τὰ Διο-

]παλαιὸν λούτριον α[ ]   10   νύcια. φ[. . . . .].αι Ἐρατοσθέ-

10   ]ωτος μετὰ τὸ π[ ]   νης περὶ Πλάτωνος ὅτι

       ].φέρεται τὸ λοιπὸν   ἕως μὲν [ἄλ]λοις ἐδίδου τὰς

τοῦ c]τίχου. τάχ᾽ ἂν οὖν τὸ   κωμωιδίας εὐδοκίμει δι᾽

       ]ςαφὲς λόγου τοῦ ἑξῆς››   αὑτοῦ δὲ πρῶτον διδάξας

τῶν c]τίχων ςαφὲς ἂν ἦν›   15   τοὺς Ῥαβδούχους καὶ γενό-

15   ]πληρωμ[. .]ο[   ]ςτ.[μενος τέταρτος ἀπεώςθη

                         πάλιν εἰς τοὺς Ληναϊκούς.

      ]..ληνογευ[   ]τ.[χρυςοκόμα φιλόμολπε. Ἀλ-

]φης[]λουτριο.[   ].[κμᾶνος ἡ ἀρχή. ὡς δίκαιον

λ]έγουσί τινες α.[20   εὐθέως καταπαλα[ί]ειν ἐστὶ

π]ροείρηται ἐν Ἱππεῦσι. κύ-   τουτ..[το]ὺς νέους διδα-

20   κν]ος ὑπὸ πτερύγων τοιόνδε   ςκαλο[. το]ῦτο βούλεται›

      ]το μὲν Ἀριστάρχειον δο-   λέγειν· κ[ατ]απαλαίεςθαι του-

      ]υν ὅτι Τερπάνδρου ἐςτὶν   τ[ ].τουc[. . . .]ὑπὸ τῶν››

ἡ] ἀρχή, Εὐφρόνιος δὲ ὅτι ἐκ   25   ]λων εὐτ.

τ]ῶν Ἴ[ω]νος μελῶν, ὁ δὲ τὴν   ]ωνται αι.[

25   π]αραπλοκὴν ὅτι ἐκ τῶν Ἀλ-   ]ι ὀλιγο[

κ]μᾶνος. ἔςτι δ᾽ ἐκ τῶν εἰς Ὁμη-   .[. . .].ν.[

ρ]ον ὕμνων. ἀλλ᾽ ἐχρῆν χορὸν   ματτοντο[

δι]δόντας[.].ον ἐπιληναι-   30   τοὐβολοῦ ς[

]ςκοπε[ῖ]ν ε.[. . .]..[]εςτιπ[]ι   δοτι εραтο[

30   ]νειθ.[   ]εται   λεγον μαλ[

      ]ςτων.[   ].[   ]ωνμα   ἐρίων τη.[βε-

       ].[   ]ωνειςτον   βραγμένην διαλελυμ[ένην

                ].τωνδε   35   εἶτα νεναγμένην πάλι[ν

              Λ]ηναϊκὸν   ].οινος ἐςτι πάντως ω[

Fr. 1 Col. i 2 .[, a hook to right on the line   3]., the right-hand end of a cross-stroke touching the top of α   7]., perhaps the overhang of ϲ   11]., the upper end of a stroke rising to right   13]., the lower end of a stroke curving down from left   15 .[, the lower part of a stroke descending below the line   16].., the lower end of a stroke curling from left and rising to right, followed by a dot level with the top of the letters and a dot below it, slightly to left, on the line   .[, a forward-sloping upright   17 .[, a trace on the line   ].[, a forward-sloping stroke, ι or the second upright of ν   18 .[, the left-hand end of a cross-stroke level with the top of the letters   28]., there are very uncertain traces which may represent the right-hand end of a cross-stroke touching the top of ο; if τ, no whole letter wanting between ϲ and ο   29 .[, on the line a hook to right   ].., prima facie οϲ acceptable, but the place is stained and partly stripped   [], a letter may have been lost in the gap before εϲτι   π[]ι, if a letter lost, ο likely   30 .[, the top of an upright   31 .[, the left-hand arc of a circle   ].[, well below the line the lower end of a stroke curving up to right (or, down to left)

Col. ii 2]., the upper part of an upright with the right-hand end of a stroke curving up from left to meet it; above apparently a circumflex. Not prima facie ῆ, εῖ, αῖ or εϊ, αϊ   4]ι, less probably ν   6]., the upper end of a stroke rising from left to touch the top of the upper end of an upright   .[, a dot level with the top of the letters   7 .[, below the line part of a stroke curving up to right   8 .[, a dot level with the top of the letters   9 ε[, less probably ϲ   10]., a short horizontal stroke on the line   13 Over ι of -μει a dot   21 ..[, the left-hand arc of a small circle, followed at an interval by the top of an upright   24 Of τ[only the left-hand end of the cross-stroke   ]., a dot level with the top of the letters   25 After τ a horizontal stroke level with the top of the letters   26 Of τ only the right-hand end of the cross-stroke against the top of α   .[, on the line a short convex stroke   27 For]ϲ perhaps ν   χο represented only by a cross-stroke with the top of a circle under its right-hand end   28 .[, the lower part of a stroke starting below the line and curving up to right, followed by a dot on the line; if one letter, η suggested, but τ.[seems possible Before ν the start of a stroke rising to right, after ν a hook to right as of ε   31 Of ϲ only the part below the cross-stroke, of ρ only the lower part of the shank, of ο[only a short arc from the upper left-hand side   33 .[, an upright   36]., the foot of an upright   Of οι only the bases

Fr. 1 Col. i 2 seq. Supplements which might be proposed as suggested by ἀπὸ Διοτίμου are δε[ύτερ]ον (or δέ[κατ]ον) | ὄν]τα, or ἄρχον]τα. But comparison with those of ll. 4–5 rules out ὄν]τα as too short and ἄρχον]τα as too long.

3 ἐφ' οὗ . . . ἐδιδάχθηϲαν. What this should mean, 'in whose year Aristophanes' first play, the Δαιταλεῖϲ, was produced', is made plain by Excerpt. π. κωμ. ii 11 Κ Ἀριϲτοφάνηϲ . . . ἐδίδαξε . . . πρῶτοϲ ἐπὶ ἄρχοντοϲ Διοτίμου διὰ Καλλιϲτράτου.

5 seqq. Catalectic anapaestic tetrameters.

In the context βα[λανεύ]ϲη⟨ι⟩ seems appropriate. 'They seat (set) the — for the bath-man to douche. . . .' Then 8 seqq. will mean: with the dirty water which he has drawn off from the sediment; say, ῥύμματοϲ αὖθιϲ ἀπαντλήϲαϲ τὸ παλαιόν | λούτριον. But if λανεν stood at the beginning of l. 7, ρυμ is insufficient for the beginning of l. 8. I do not know whether ϲμῆγμα is found (as ῥύμμα is, e.g. schol. Nic. *Al.* 96) for the deposit left by the material used as a substitute for soap.

ἐν λειψυδρίαι που 'during a drought', but I do not see the effect of που in this place.

λούτριον see on 17 seqq., below.

10 seqq. I suppose, ο]ὐ φέρεται. 'After — the remainder of the verse is wanting in the manuscript(s).' Cf. schol. Eur. *Phoen.* 375 ὁ ϲτίχοϲ οὗτοϲ ἔν τιϲιν οὐ φέρεται, schol. T *Il.* xxiv 420 τοῦτο δὲ τὸ ἡμιϲτίχιον οὐδὲ φέρεται.

12 seqq. Perhaps τὸ | νῦν] ἀϲαφέϲ. The sense appears to be: Perhaps the obscurity of what is said in the following could have been obviated by . . . .

15 πε]πληρωμ[έν]ο[

17 seqq. λούτριον occurs at Aristoph. *Knights* 1401 with a scholium τὸ λοῦτρον, τὸ ἀπόλουμα καὶ ῥυπαρόν, ὅ ἐϲτι τὸ ἀπόλουτρον. Hence there is a possibility that ἀπ[όλουμα or ἀπ[όλουτρον is to be recognized in l. 18, but ἀπ[όνιπτρον is another alternative.

The word is cited also from Aristophanes' lost *Ἥρωεϲ* (Pollux vii 167, x 78).

προείρηται ἐν *Ἱππεῦϲι* 'has already been noted in the commentary on the *Knights*'. Similarly at

Peace 1014 καὶ ἐν τοῖς Ἀχαρνεῦϲιν ἔφαμεν refers to a comment on *Acharnians* 894, at *Wasps* 1206 εἴρηται περὶ Φαΰλλου ἐν τοῖς Ἀχαρνεῦϲιν to one on *Acharnians* 214.

Two inferences seem to be justifiable: (1) that the present text is a commentary on a play of Aristophanes; (2) that this play was subsequent to the *Knights* (his fourth).[1]

19 seqq. δο[κο]ῦν seems unavoidable, but I can see no normal Greek expression for what must have been meant: Aristarchus takes the view that the lemma is the first words of Terpander's poems. The position of μέν seems to imply that τοιόνδε (perhaps followed by τι in the next line) is part of the lemma. The form of Εὐφρόνιος δέ implies something of the form Ἀρίϲταρχος μὲν δοκεῖ to precede.

Aristarchus and Euphronius are each cited more than two dozen times in the extant scholia on Aristophanes, Aristarchus mainly on *Frogs*, Euphronius on *Wasps* and *Birds*.

Ion of Chios referred to by Aristophanes in *Acharnians* (l. 835, on which the comment gives a list of his works), and quoted, according to the scholiast (τοῦτο Ἴωνός ἐϲτιν . . .), at *Frogs* 706.

ὁ τὴν παραπλοκήν presumably 'the author of the Παραπλοκή'. As literary terms παραπλοκή and παραπλέκειν are used to refer to the insertion of portions of one text in another, often what we should call 'quotation', as, for example, schol. V *Birds* 1376 ἐκ δὲ τῶν αὐτοῦ Κινηϲίου παραπλοκὴν ἔχει,[2] Hermog. π. ἰδ. ii 4 (320 seqq. W) τὰς παραπλοκὰς τῶν ποιημάτων ἐν λόγωι, εἰ ἐκ διαϲτάϲεως παραπλέκοιτο τὰ ποιήματα, sometimes in a wider sense of combining two texts, as in Hyp. vii of Aristoph. *Clouds* τὰ μὲν γὰρ περιήιρηται, τὰ δὲ παραπέπλεκται, of the alternative versions of the play. (Of a pervading characteristic of a composition Strabo 34.)

For the ellipse of γράψας or the like cf. schol. T *Il.* xix 326 ὁ τὴν μικρὰν Ἰλιάδα.

ἔϲτι δ' ἐκ τῶν εἰς Ὅμηρον ὕμνων. That a 'hymn to Homer' was ever composed (whether by Alcman or another) is not to be believed, still less more than one. What is meant is obviously τῶν εἰς Ὅμηρον ἀναφερομένων ὕμνων. The words κύκνος ὑπὸ πτερύγων are in fact found at *hy. Hom.* xxi 1. But this does not prove the other attributions wrong and Professor Fraenkel regards that to Ion as very likely in view of *Frogs* 706 (see above), in the same metre.

27 seqq. Prima facie trochaic tetrameters.

ἀλλ' ἐχρῆν χορὸν διδόντας τὸν ἐπὶ Ληναίωι ϲκοπεῖν. . . . 'But in assigning a chorus to a competitor at the Lenaea, they had to consider (or 'should have considered'). . . . Who is 'they'? If the decipherment is correct, it must be the successive archons. I should have expected διδόντα, but the context may have contained a reason for the plural.

ἐπὶ Ληναίωι in place of an adjective as *Acharn.* l. 504 οὑπὶ Ληναίωι . . . ἀγών, Law *ap.* Dem. *Meid.* 10 ἡ ἐπὶ Ληναίωι πομπή. Or the adjective ἐπιλήναιος itself may have been used, cf., e.g., schol. *Acharn.* 202 (where it has been corrected away), I.G. ii² Add. 8346 ii 46.

After ϲκοπεῖν something expressing 'the qualifications of the applicant' would be suitable, but εἰ cannot be read.

Col. ii 1 seq. In spite of what I say in the app. crit. it is tempting to guess Λη[ν]αϊκά.

5 ϲυμμαχ[. It may be suspected that hereabouts there is reference to the fact that strangers were not present at the Lenaea in any number (cf. *Acharn.* 504 seqq. αὐτοὶ γάρ ἐϲμεν οὑπὶ Ληναίωι τ' ἀγών | κοὔπω ξένοι πάρειϲιν· οὔτε γὰρ φόροι | ἥκουϲιν οὔτ' ἐκ τῶν πόλεων οἱ ξύμμαχοι c. scholl.), or alternatively that they were present at the city Dionysia.

7 The angle of the stroke at the beginning of the line seems irreconcilable with a *diple* as made elsewhere. I suppose, therefore, that πρ]αγματ[ευ-ϲομεν- is part of the comment, not of a lemma, though Aristophanes has this verb at *Clouds* 256.

10 seq. Presumably in his work, περὶ τῆς ἀρχαίας κωμωιδίας, in not less than twelve books.

---

[1] This is not unquestionable. As far as I have been able to ascertain, if a note on play A refers to a note on play B, as a rule play B was produced before play A. That is, as a rule commentaries seem to follow the order of production. But notes at *Birds* 749, 1379 (produced 414 B.C.) refer to notes on *Frogs* 13, etc., 1437 (produced 405 B.C.), and a note at *Lysistrata* 801 (produced 411 B.C.) refers to a note (lost) on *Ecclesiazusae* 303 (believed to have been produced in 392 B.C.). Similarly notes at *Acharnians* 381 and 961 refer to notes on *Knights* 137 and 95 (produced in the following year). Aristophanes' first and second plays were Δαιταλεῖς and Βαβυλώνιοι. His third, *Acharnians*, obviously does not enter into the question.

[2] At *Peace* 775 I take the scholiast to say αὕτη δὲ ⟨παρα⟩πλοκή ἐϲτι. καὶ ἔλαθε 'this is a quotation. It was not recognized.'

11 Πλάτωνος Twenty-eight (or more) names of comedies attributed to him are known, none named 'Ραβδοῦχοι either of Plato or another.

12 ἄλλοις ἐδίδου As shown by the contrasting δι' αὐτοῦ... διδάξας, this is equivalent to 'got produced for him by ...'.[1] So of Aristophanes Excerpt. π. κωμ. ii 11 K ἐδίδαξε δὲ ... διὰ Καλλιστράτου, τὰς μὲν γὰρ πολιτικὰς τούτωι φασὶν αὐτὸν διδόναι, τὰ δὲ κατ' Εὐριπίδου καὶ Cωκράτους Φιλωνίδηι.

13 εὐδοκίμει 'was placed', cf. schol. *Clouds* 528 ἄριστ' ἠκουσάτην· ἀντὶ τοῦ ηὐδοκίμησαν, οὐ γὰρ ἐνίκησαν, ἐπεὶ δεύτερος ἐκρίθη.

15 seq. It is to be presumed that the note beginning in l. 10 has some relevance to the preceding lemma. I cannot guess what it is. What seems to emerge from the information given about Plato is that of the five comic poets allowed to compete at the City Dionysia only three were placed, the unsuccessful fourth (and fifth?) were allowed to compete, that is, I suppose, established a claim to a chorus, at the ensuing Lenaea about nine months later.

18 New fragment of Alcman. Of Apollo?

19 seqq. Trochaic tetrameters.

I suppose that the commentator has changed the statement in the lemma from the active to the passive form in order to obviate the ambiguity of the subject's being in the same case as the object. δίκαιόν ἐστι διδασκάλους καταπαλαίειν τούτους τοὺς νέους means δίκαιόν ἐστι καταπαλαίεσθαι τούτους τοὺς [νέους] ὑπὸ τῶν ... [διδασκά]λων. But I cannot explain the absence of the article before διδασκαλο[in the lemma nor guess what occupied the space between τῶν and διδασκά]λων in the comment.

30 τοὐβολοῦ '(for) a penny' cf., e.g., *Knights* 945 τοῖσι πολλοῖς τοὐβολοῦ, 'cheap'.

31 Eratosthenes mentioned again?

32 seq. ἐρίων suggests the possibility that μαλ[represents μαλλός or some case of it.

33 seq. βε|βραγμένην The explanation διαλελυμένην 'scattered' shows that βράττειν in its use 'winnow' (or an extension of this) is to be recognized. The compound ἀναβε|βραγμένην may have occurred, cf. Aristot. *Meteor.* 368ᵇ29 τὰ ἐν τοῖς λίκνοις ἀναβραττόμενα.

I find no warrant for the γ and suppose c should be substituted.

The *diple* should have been inserted one line higher.

35 εἶτα νεναγμένην πάλιν 'and then made into a pile again'. In this verb, though γ(κ) is sometimes found in the relevant forms, c seems preferred. But there appears to be confusion in the perfect forms with νέω, meaning to 'heap'. Cf. *Clouds* 1203, *Ecclesiazusae* 838, 840.

Col. ii 36–Fr. 2 (Col. iii?) 1 seqq. A reference to the mixture of water and wine for drinking.

5 seqq. φά]κους, φάκου[c, τοὺς φάκο[υc. A note on lentil porridge, elsewhere referred to as φακῆ by Aristophanes (10 times), but φάκοι as here at Pherec. Κοριαννώ (fr. 67, 3 seq.).

17 Ambiguous, but not improbably ἡ Τρικόρυ[(ν)θος or the derived adjective, as at *Lysistr.* 1031 ἐμπίδος Τρικορυσίας.

20 Ἑρμι[ππος in some form? This writer of comedies is not infrequently quoted in the extant scholia.

21 seq. τὴν ἀρχ[ὴν ... Αἰ]|cχύλου.

22 From the position of the *diple* it is to be inferred that 23 seq. are a lemma from the comedy, not a quotation from Aeschylus. To be sure, they might be both at once.

---

[1] Professor Fraenkel adduces in this connexion the entry in Suidas: Ἀρκάδας μιμούμενοι· ἐπὶ τῶν ἑτέροις πονούντων. οἱ γὰρ Ἀρκάδες μαχιμώτατοι Ἑλλήνων γενόμενοι ἰδίαι μὲν οὐδένα ἐνίκησαν, ἑτέροις δὲ συμμαχοῦντες πολλούς. ταύτηι δὲ τῆι παροιμίαι κέχρηται Πλάτων ἐν Πεισάνδρωι. διὰ γὰρ τὸ τὰς κωμωιδίας αὐτὸς ποιῶν ἄλλοις παρέχειν διὰ πενίαν, Ἀρκάδας μιμεῖσθαι ἔφη and ingeniously suggests that Eratosthenes derived his information from the παράβασις of the Πείσανδρος.

Fr. 2

```
       ]οϲκεκραμ[
       ]παραχε[
       ]φηϲινε[
       ] κεκραμ[
  5    ] ταλλα[
          /
       ] κουϲπ[
       ] νυνφ[
       ] φακο.[
       ] δεφα[
 10    ] τουϲφακο[
          /
       ] προϲτηνε.[
       ] ϊναδραμα[
       ] ταιχοροϲκ.[
       ] πρωτοντ[
          /
 15    ] μενουμ[
       ] μιαναρα[
       ] ητρικορυ[
       ] οτιτονδ[
       ] τονκω[
 20    ] ταδερμι[
       ] δετηναρχ[
       ] ϲχυλου α[
          /
       ] παϲαδηπα[
       ] διρκηϲαγχ[
 25       ]τ[
```

.   .   .

Fr. 2 (Col. iii?) I can trace no fibres across from fr. 1 into fr. 2, but there are some grounds for believing that they broke apart at a 'joint'. There appears to be a certain congruity in the contents of fr. 1 ii 36 and fr. 2, 1–4

8 .[, a dot on the line   13 .[, perhaps the lower end of the loop of α

2738. Commentary on an Old Comedy

The following scrap, which I have taken to refer to a particular part of a particular dance, resembles the general run of notes on Old Comedy closely enough to be reasonably assigned to such a source, though I suppose this is not the only possibility.

As col. ii is almost entirely occupied by the comment on a single lemma, the only evidence that survives about the articulation of the commentary is the 'colon' in col. ii 15 and the διπλῆ ὠβελιςμένη followed by a line ἐν ἐκθέςει at col. iii 4 seq. There are three syntactical divisions marked by high stops, col. ii, 1, 7, 12, but these seem to be rather capriciously used. There is none between ποειν ϲκλη, l. 3.

The script is a smallish book-hand of a type assigned to the early second century.

Col. i	Col. ii	Col. iii	Col. ii
	πυρριχιζων·ενδεαιξινευ	ρ[	πυρριχίζων, ἐν δὲ Αἰξὶν Εὐ-
	π..[....]τομαλακηνκε	ι̣[	πόλ[ιδος] τὸ μαλακὴν κε-
	[.].[.[..].ηναθηνανποεινϲκλη	χ[	λ]εύειν τὴν Ἀθηνᾶν ποεῖν. ϲκλη-
	[.]. ∴ .[ ]π̣ό.ουντ[..]τουαγροι	ϲϵ[	ρ]ῳς ποιοῦντο[ϲ] τοῦ ἀγροί-
5	κουτοϲχηματ.ϲαθηναϲ	κ[	κου τὸ ϲχῆμα τῆϲ Ἀθηνᾶϲ
	οδιδ[.]ϲκ.....κελευϲενμα		ὁ διδ[ά]ϲκαλοϲ ἐκέλευϲεν μα-
	λακ[]ῳϲ......ιειν·ωϲουν	and the beginnings	λακῶϲ αὐτὸ ποιεῖν. ὡϲ οὖν
	οαρ[..].[.].[.]νη[.].ω‘τριτογε	of two more separate	ὁ Ἀρ[ιϲ]τ[ο]φ[ά]νη[ϲ] τῶι Τριτογε-
	νεια[]....ε.ιθετω‘ηρκε	lines below, opposite	νεια[]μόνωι ἐπιθέτωι ἠρκέ-
10	ϲθηκαιοκρα.[.]ν..τω‘γοργο	the ends of Col. ii	ϲθη καὶ ὁ Κρατ[ῖ]νοϲ τῶι Γοργο-
	..ακον.οδο[[κ̅τ]]α.[ ]..κεϲθη	10 and 12	.ρακον.οδοκα.[ ] ἠρκέϲθη
	τ[.]αυτο̣δηλουντ.[.]..αγμα·		τ[ὸ] αὐτὸ δηλοῦντ.[.] πρᾶγμα,
	ο̣τιαποκλειν.[.]η‘κεφαλη[ ]		ὅτι ἀποκλιν.[τ]ῆι κεφαλῆι
	...[ ]..[.]υϲχημ.πο.[].[ ]		...[ ] θϵ[ο]ῦ ϲχῆμα πο.[]..
15	λ..ι̣[ ].[].ται: .μοι[ ]		λ..ι̣[ ].[]ϵται. κτλ.
	]μυνο̣ι̣[		
	].ϵν[		
	].[		

The papyrus is broken, warped, and wrinkled, and in places rubbed or skinned. It is often possible to be fairly sure of what was meant and even of what was written, but I cannot in all cases accommodate the supposed letters to the surviving ink.

Heading. Above Col. ii a line in a thick cursive, beginning αι but otherwise too broken and discontinuous to decipher.

Col. i Extreme ends of about a dozen discontinuous lines.

Col. ii 2 πολ[Of ο, which is unusually distant from π, only the upper part; of λ only faint traces of the upper part of the right-hand stroke   3]..[faint specks on either side of a short upright; neither λ]ενειν nor λ]ευcαι in any way suggested   Of τ only the extreme lower end of the stalk   4].˙.˙.[in the line a flat stroke, followed by the tops of two slightly forward-sloping strokes and then confused ink, perhaps a corrected or cancelled letter. Superscribed in the same hand what could be taken for a small ω and, even more doubtfully, c   9 Of μ only the right-hand stroke preceded by faint dispersed specks   11 The first letter represented by an upright with a small projection to left at its top   Between ν and ο what looks like the left-hand stroke of υ   .[a dot just above mid-letter   12 .[the lower part of an upright, apparently slightly convex   13 .[ω suggested, but perhaps ο. possible   14 ...[, dispersed specks, followed by a cross-stroke, level with the top of the letters, having part of an upright below its right-hand end   .[].., the top of a tall upright, followed after a small gap by what resembles the tips of ω with a suspended ι against the right-hand tip   15 After λ (for which δ may be possible) perhaps elements of the top half of ε touching the left-hand end of the loop of φ   16 Of υ only elements of the arms; of ϙ only the flattened upper left-hand side; what I have rendered ν[might be divided between two letters, e.g. ρα

Col. iii 4 θ[perhaps not ruled out

Col. ii 1 πυρριχίζων 'dancing the πυρρίχη', which is ἐνόπλιος ... ὄρχηςις (schol. Aristoph. *Av.* 1169). It does not appear to be different from the dance referred to in *Nub.* 988 seq., on which there is a note (not in R, V): Τριτογενείης· εἶδος ὀρχήςεως ἣ καλεῖται ἐνόπλιος, διὰ δὲ τὸ εἰς Ἀθηνᾶν ταύτην τελεῖсθαι Τριτογένεια κέκληται.

1 seqq. I suppose the meaning to be 'In Eupolis, *Goats*, the instruction to make the Athena suave (is a corroboration of, example of, what I say).' Since μαλακὴν ποιεῖν does not seem to be different from μαλακῶς ποιεῖν, presumably τὴν Ἀθηνᾶν is a short way of expressing τὸ сχῆμα τῆς Ἀθηνᾶς and the reference is to the performance of a figure in the dance.

For сκληρῶς cf. Athenaeus 667b (with a reference to Plato, Ζεὺς κακούμενος) μὴ сκληρὰν ἔχειν τὴν χεῖρα μέλλοντα κοτταβίζειν.

3 seqq. I cannot verify the possibility which may be thought of, that there was a correction of -ρον to -ρωс—in fact, I do not see how -ρον could be reconciled with what is now visible—but there does not appear to be any doubt about the sense required. γάρ might also have been expected, but I do not think there is room for it to have been written.

There is no doubt about the oblique stroke above πο-. It is the solitary accent and it is wrong. τοῦ ἀγροίκου ... ὁ διδάсκαλος: from the fragments of the *Αἶγες* already known it was inferred that a theme of the play was the instruction of a rustic by a teacher of music and letters, called (according to Quintilian, *Inst. or.* i 10, 17) Prodamus. See Eupol. frr. 2, 3, 11, 13, 17, 303.

8 seqq. 'Aristophanes was satisfied with Τριτογένεια by itself as an epithet.' I have no clear idea what this tells us; that Aristophanes expected the allusion to the Athena-figure in the dance to be plain? If *Nub.* 989 is the place referred to, which looks likely, ἀμελῆι τῆς Τριτογενείης may have been understood to mean 'fails to perform the prescribed evolution', 'doesn't bother about the dance'.

10 seqq. Γοργο.ρακον.οδοκα.[This word, which was 'good enough' (no doubt as an allusion to Athena) 'for Kratinus', should be recoverable, but I can think of nothing nearer than Γοργοδρακοντοδόκα (the feminine ending as in Γοργολόφα Aristoph. *Eq.* 1181, Γοργοφόνα Eur. *Ion* 1478) 'grim-dragon-awaiting (goddess)', and this was certainly not written.

τὸ αὐτὸ δηλοῦντι πρᾶγμα 'the same' as what? I should have supposed, as what is asserted in ll. 13 seqq. But though there is some doubt about the exact form of this, I see nothing above which could be thought exactly equivalent to it.

ὅτι 'namely, that ...'.

ἀποκλιν-ων is too much for the space, -ω gives no sense, -οι or -ον is left. Which is chosen depends on the exact form of the end of the clause, which I cannot make out. I suppose the general sense to be: the goddess-figure (is performed) with the head sloping, i.e. in an attitude of expectancy. At the beginning of l. 14, though I cannot verify τὸ τῆς, it seems unavoidable; at the end, I have failed to elicit any appropriate form of πο(ι)εῖν.

2739. List of Plays by Cratinus

The bottom of a column containing part of a list of plays by Cratinus written in an upright hand of, I suppose, the second century.

On the back is part of an isolated line (written in the opposite direction by a hand that will not be much later) which may be *Il.* ii 778 or xvii 1.

```
      .      .     .                    .      .      .
     ].λαια[                          Π]υλαία[
     ] δηλιαδ[                        ]Δηλιάδ[εϲ
     ]  πλουτο[                       ]  Πλοῦτο[ι
     ]  νεμεϲιϲ[                      ]  Νέμεϲιϲ[
  5  ]  δραπετι[                      ]  Δραπέτι[δεϲ
     ]  βουκολο[                      ]  Βουκόλο[ι
```

Since the order of the titles preserved is not alphabetical and will not readily be presumed to be arbitrary, the question arises whether it is chronological. **663** records an order in which Cratinus' Διονυϲαλέξανδροϲ is '8th' and since it is there implied that that play was produced in 430 B.C. it is thought impossible that it should be chronologically 8th. We do not know that our list (which may or may not have had a marginal numeration—too little is left of the left-hand margin to say) represents the same order, but the probability is that there was not more than one accepted order and in that case Διονυϲαλέξανδροϲ was not alphabetically 8th either.

The necessary conclusion, that the accepted order was neither alphabetical nor chronological, is borne out by similar evidence about the plays of other dramatists, see Pearson, *Fragments of Sophocles* I xvi.

3 Fragments of the Πλοῦτοι in a papyrus published in Mél. Bidez 603 seqq. and PSI 1212.

4 The date of Νέμεϲιϲ, stated in schol. Aristoph. *Av.* 521 to be a good deal later than 414 B.C. but containing a gibe at Pericles, d. 429 B.C. (fr. 111), gets no light from its position in this list.

2740. SCHOLIA ON OLD COMEDY [See Addendum, p. 102]

In the comedy to which the following comments apply a speaking part was taken, as appears from fr. 1, 13, by Phormion, the Athenian admiral. The only other comedy, so far as I know, of which this was true is the Ταξίαρχοι of Eupolis. The chorus of that play must be presumed to have consisted of these officers (although there were annually no more than ten), who are mostly described as corps commanders (Aristot. Ἀθ. πολ. c. 61, 3, Pollux viii 94) but sometimes held naval commands (Xen. *Hell.* i 6, 29, al.). The chorus of the play here annotated would, I think, be guessed on the strength of fr. 2 ii 21 to have been composed of sailors. I find nothing in the rest of what is preserved which might afford a clue to identification.

The layout of the text appears to have been theoretically: lemma projecting 1–2 letters to left and separated by a blank from the following, and, if it starts within a line, from the preceding, comment; the beginnings of both lemma and comment signalized by a paragraphus under the first letters of the line in which they start. But I am not sure how accurately in respect of the blanks the intention has been carried out.

The text is written in narrow columns, in lines containing *c.* 16 or *c.* 19 letters or their equivalent, in a medium-sized upright hand which might, I think, be dated as early as the end of the first century.

Fr. 1

```
        ].·.[                          ].·.[
      ] πτω[                         ] πτω[
      ] χρω.[                        ] χρω.[
      ] δελεγ[                       ] δελεγ[
  5   ]δεινεστ[                      ]δειvεcτ[
      ] περις[                       ] περιc[
      ]τουτουσοφοκλεο[               ]τουτου Cοφοκλέο[υc
      ].εισνινεισφθορ[              ]θεις νιν εἰς φθορ[
      ]μενταιταδαλλα[               ]μενται ταδαλλα[
 10   ]σοφοκλεουσες[                 ]Cοφοκλέους εc[
      ]τηρεωσδοκω [                  ]Τηρέωc δοκῶ [
     .]οσαρκετονλογω[               .]οσαρκετον λόγω[ ἀν-
      ]τιτουαμφοτεροι[              ]τὶ τοῦ ἀμφοτεροι[ οὐ-
     ].οισθαρημοιτουν.[            ]κ οἶcθ' Ἄρη μοι τοὖνο[-
 15  .]α αρησοφορμιω[              μ]α; Ἄρηc ὁ Φορμίω[ν ἐ-
      ]πεκαλειτο κοκ[               ]πεκαλεῖτο. κόκ[κυ
     ].οι αντιτουπριν[             ].οι ἀντὶ τοῦ πρὶν [
      ]κοκκυ ηδυστρ[               ]κόκκυ. ηδυcτρ[
      ]θαιπλ.ηνεστ.[             .]θαι πλ.ηνεcτι[
 20  ].μισθον[].ντ[               ].μιcθον[]αντ[
      ]π.φ[                         ]ποφ[
```

Fr. 1 1 The foot of an upright serifed to right, followed by the base of a circle with a horizontal stroke to right; perhaps]‚ω[, or three letters represented   3 .[, the left-hand side of ε or less probably c   7 Below]τ a short slightly backward-sloping stroke, not apparently the foot of the letter   8 Of]θ only the upper right-hand side   9 Of]μ only the right-hand stroke   Below ε there is a trace which, if not casual ink, could be taken for the right-hand tip of a paragraphus 14 Of]κ only the right-hand ends of the upper and lower arms   17]., the extreme right-hand end of a cross-stroke touching the top of o   18 Above and to left of first κ the end of a cross-stroke rising gently to right   19 Between λ and η a cusp on the line, above the left-hand side of which the left-hand arc of a circle with a dot to right opposite its centre   20]., perhaps the underside of the loop and the tip and tail of the right-hand stroke of α   Of]α only the end of the tail rising to the left-hand upright of ν

Fr. 1 7 seqq. No paragraphus is now visible below l. 7, but I think this must be because the surface is damaged. The projection (ἔκθεcιc) implies that ll. 7 and 8 and part at least of 9 must be lemma. This lemma might begin in l. 6 (so that the articulation of τουτου is ambiguous) and may (or, if a paragraphus is rightly descried under l. 9, must) end in l. 9.

8 From νιν, which is not a constituent of the vocabulary of comedy, it appears that the lemma itself contains a quotation. It comes presumably from the *Tereus* of Sophocles.

εἰς φθορ[άν looks acceptable. Preceded by προ|θείς?

9 seqq.]μενται must be part of the lemma. I can arrive at no explanation of its meaning. Whether ταδαλλα, however articulated, is lemma or comment I am uncertain, but the comment, which is marked as ending in l. 11 and clearly includes l. 10, might have extended back so far. I suppose its tenor was: the lemma is a quotation from (reference to, parody of) Sophocles *Tereus*. For a quotation cited in a form like τὰ δ᾽ ἄλλα . . . Cοφοκλέους ἐcτὶν ἐκ Τηρέωc cf. schol. Aristoph. *Vesp.* 1239 παραθεὶc τὰ τοῦ Κρατίνου ἐκ Χειρώνων, Κλειταγόραc ᾄιδειν κτλ., ib. 1074 ὁ cτίχοc Εὐριπίδου ἐκ Cθενεβοίαc.

There is no blank before δοκω but appears to be one after it. δοκῶ as part of the comment is not favourable to the hypothesis just offered.

12 seq. Before]ο there appears to be room for no more than a narrow letter.

The words which can be elicited from these letters (e.g. -οcαρκε, -αρκετον) are unlikely in themselves and the comment does not seem to apply to them, except in so far as -ετον and -γω could be taken for duals.

ἀρκετόc is found in glossaries as an interpretation of ἱκανόc. If it should be recognized here, I am presumably wrong in marking it as lemma.

13 seqq. The Phormion who, the comment implies, is speaking is no doubt the Athenian admiral. (Four other persons of this name alluded to in Old Comedy, schol. Aristoph. *Pax* 347.) References to him in comedy are not rare, but as a character in a play I cannot find that he occurs elsewhere except in the Ταξίαρχοι of Eupolis (fr. 250).

16 seq. κόκκυ is interpreted as ὀλίγον (schol. Aristoph. *Av.* 50), τὸ ἐλάχιcτον (Hesych. in v.), οὐδὲ κόκκυ· οὐδὲ βραχύ (Bekk. Anecd. Gr. 105) and as Attic for ταχύ (Et. Mag., Suid. in v.). In Aristophanes it is used as a signal to start an action (κ., μέθεcθε *Ran.* 1384, κ., ψωλοὶ πεδίονδε *Av.* 507). In the comment here I should guess the interpretation given was 'before (you) can say "knife" ', but I have no convincing completion of the lemma, little as is missing.

18 seqq. I suppose c]θαι is likely, but I see no clue to the completion and articulation of what precedes, and I have failed to make anything out of the letters which follow, which I think must be still part of the lemma.

20 ᾳντ[has a fair chance of representing ἀντὶ τοῦ, the beginning of the comment.

Fr. 2

Col. i　　　　　　　　　　　　　　Col. ii

. · . · · · · · · · · · ·

Stripped

]μ.ν[

].ọ.[

Stripped

  ,,

  ,,

  ,,

]..ατι.[

]οϲ εϲτηκαϲηδ[

]..ξυνθημαν[

10　]αϲονκαιγνω[

]πληϲιοναν[

].ωιπληϲιον.[

]ντοϲυνθημα[

]. νητονδιαλ[

15　]καιμιϲωγεπρ[　　　　　　　　] γο.[

]νφορμιωναι.[ ]　　　　　　πα..ρ.[

]τεπρωτηνελ[　　　　　　　]_τιτουεμ[

].υλακην ειτου　　　　　γαρουκεπιϲταμαι[

]μονδητ.γωπορ　　　5　τοπεζηβαδιζω[

20　]ϲ αντιτουχω　　　　　　γαρουκεπιϲταμα[

]ηϲαπλωϲοπερ　　　　　παυϲειραινωνημ[

]οιατεχνωϲλε　　　　　πρωιραϲ ειωθαϲιλ[

]ϲε.ωκ...ειν　　　　　οεκπρωραϲμηρ[

]ονι τουτουμνη　　10　εκτενειϲουντονϲ[

25　]κ..τηλεκλει　　　　ϲκον αντιτουτοϲκ[

]ω ϲλωπο

Fr. 2 Col. i 1 Before ν presumably η or π, but either anomalous. γι, which the ink most suggests, precluded　　2]., ε or ϲ　　Of ọ only the lower part; θ perhaps possible　.[, the feet of converging strokes; possibly κ　　7].., a dot off the line, followed by the lower part of an upright descending below the line　　9].., a stroke on the line coming from left to touch a slightly convex upright, perhaps]αι, followed by what seem to be elements of a concave bracket　　11 Of]π only faint traces of the cross-stroke　　12]., the right-hand end of a cross-stroke touching the top of ω

Fr. 2

Col. i   Col. ii

.   .   .   .

Seven fragmentary or lost verses

]οс ἕcτηκαcηδ[

].. ξύνθημαν[

10   ]αcον καὶ γνω[

]πληcίον αν[

].ωι πληcίον .[

]ντο cυνθημα[

]. νὴ τὸν Δίαλ[

15   ]καὶ μιcῶ γε πρ[   ]   γο.[

]ν Φορμίωναι.[ ]   πα. .ρι[ἀν-

]τε πρώτην ελ[τὶ τοῦ εμ[

]φυλακήν. εἶτου   γὰρ οὐκ ἐπίcταμαι [παρὰ

]μον δῆτ' ἐγὼ πορ-   5   τὸ πεζῇ βαδίζω [νεῖν

20   ]c ἀντὶ τοῦ χω-   γὰρ οὐκ ἐπίcταμα[ι. οὐ

]ηc ἁπλῶc ὅπερ   παύcει ῥαίνων ἡμ[ᾶc, οὐκ

]οι ἀτεχνῶc λε-   πρώιραc; εἰώθαcι λ[έγειν·

]c ἐγὼ κλαίειν   ὁ ἐκ πρῴραc, μὴ ῥ[αῖνε .

]ονι. τούτου μνη-   10   ἐκτενεῖc οὖν τὸν c[κελί-

25   μονεύει] καὶ Τηλεκλεί-   cκον ἀντὶ τοῦ τὸ c[κέλοc

δηc   ]ὼc λωπο-

Col. ii δύτου

Above and below *o* curly strokes to which I cannot attach any meaning   .[, the left-hand side of a circle   14]., the right-hand side of a circle   For λ[I cannot rule out ν   15 Of ρ[only the top of the loop and the extreme lower end of the stalk   16 .[, the lower left-hand arc of a circle with a hook to left at its upper end, and scattered ink above and to right. The fibres may be in disorder   17 Of λ[only the apex   18]., φ suggested by a trace above the general level   19 After τ I should guess ε, not α, but no letter could be verified   23 Between ε and ω I cannot tell whether γ or τ is intended   After κ level with the top of the letters the tip of a stroke descending to right, at the same level the tip of another stroke, than a dot on the line; λαι seems acceptable but cannot be verified

Col. ii 1 .[, a dot on the line   2 After α the foot of an upright turning to right; ι sometimes so made   Before ρ a tall upright with traces of ink across its top; τ not particularly suggested

Fr. 2 Col. i Through loss, along with the left-hand margin, of the guidance afforded by ἔκθεϲιϲ of the lemma and by the paragraphi, the only external indication of the distinction between lemma and comment is now the blank spaces left between them. As for internal evidence, (i) some words and phrases are many times more likely to occur in comment than in lemma, (ii) if a word occurs twice in the same neighbourhood, it is likely that its first occurrence is in the lemma, its second in the comment. But these clues are not enough to enable all ambiguities to be resolved.

Fr. 2 Col. i 8 seq. There is a blank before ἔϲτηκαϲηδ[and apparently before ξύνθημαν[. If these are both beginnings of lemmas, as the second certainly is, a short comment must be supposed lost between them. But perhaps it is likelier that the first is comment and that the preceding lemma is what is represented by]οϲ.

9 seqq. ξύνθημαν[to πληϲίον appear to be the subject of comment in ll. 11–14. ἀν[|τὶ τοῦ is perhaps to be recognized in ll. 11 seq., but there is no more space between -ον and αν[than between, e.g., -ον and καὶ in the previous line.

14 seqq. I cannot determine how far the lemma beginning νή extends. The first obvious blank up to ἀντὶ τοῦ in l. 20 is between φ and ο of φορμιων, l. 16. Perhaps this should be regarded as misplaced by one letter, so that the comment starts with Φορμίων(-). It may end with φυλακήν, l. 18, after which there appears to be a blank, though damage makes it hard to be certain. At any rate it has ended by l. 19, which is recognizable on internal evidence as lemma, running as far as the blank followed by what is obviously the beginning of comment in l. 20.

14 seq. Quite likely νὴ τὸν Δί’, ἀλ|λά, as often in Aristophanes, e.g. *Plut.* 202; v. Blaydes's collections.

15 I have articulated as I think most likely, but other articulations are easily thought of.

17 seq. πρώτην . . . φυλακήν presumably go together. They may have already occurred in ll. 15 seq. For the number of night-watches see Macan's note on Hdt. ix 51.

18 Very likely I ought to indicate εἴτου as lemma as well as 19 seq.

20 seqq. Although I cannot see any particular guidance from blanks, I am inclined to think that the following interpretation will not be far from the truth: ἀντὶ τοῦ χω|ρὶϲ -ηϲ. **ἁπλῶϲ·** ὅπερ | Ἀττικοὶ ἀτεχνῶϲ λέ|γουϲιν.

For ἁπλῶϲ, which is found twice in Aristophanes as against ἀτεχνῶϲ more than a dozen times, cf., e.g., schol. *Plut.* 109 (ἀτεχνῶϲ ἀντὶ τοῦ ἁπλῶϲ); for (οἱ) Ἀττικοὶ λέγουϲι schol. *Pax* 11, *Plut.* 72.

24 seqq. For the form cf., e.g., schol. Aristoph. *Vesp.* 592 μνημονεύει δὲ αὐτοῦ καὶ Πλάτων ἐν Πειϲάνδρωι. Teleicleides mentioned one Androcles as a βαλλαντιοτόμοϲ (fr. 15 ex schol. Aristoph. *Vesp.* 1187), perhaps in his ʻΗϲίοδοι. A βαλλαντιοτόμοϲ is presumably not the same as a λωποδύτηϲ, though they are classed together in Aristoph. *Ran.* 772. The only name of a λωποδύτηϲ I can supply is Orestes, *Av.* 712, 1490, *Ach.* 1167.

Fr. 2 Col. ii 3 seqq. Some phrase like κιθαρίζειν γὰρ οὐκ ἐπίϲταται (ἐπίϲταμαι) Aristoph. *Vesp.* 959, (989), ϲκάπτειν γὰρ οὐκ ἐπίϲταμαι *Av.* 1432, and explained, as by the scholia there, by reference to the saying πεζῆι βαδίζω, νεῖν γὰρ οὐκ ἐπίϲταμαι Apostol. *Cent.* xiv 16a.

6 seqq. 'Stop splashing us, you in the bows.'

οὐ παύϲει; as an imperative, cf., e.g., Aristoph. *Lysist.* 383.

ὁ ἐκ πρώιραϲ as a vocative, cf., e.g., πρόϊθ’ ὡϲ τὸ πρόϲθεν ὀλίγον, ἡ κανηφόροϲ *Acharn.* 242, ὁ παῖϲ ἀκολούθει δεῦρο *Ran.* 521.

9 I suppose οὐκ ἐκτενεῖϲ . . . ;

10 seq. ϲκελίϲκοϲ otherwise only at *Eccles.* 1167.

2741. COMMENTARY ON EUPOLIS, *Μαρικᾶϲ*

There would have been no difficulty in identifying the subject of the following remains of a commentary, even if its title were not partially preserved on the back of the roll in which it is written, since there recur there four ancient quotations to which the name of Eupolis is attached, two of them further specifying the play, *Μαρικᾶϲ* (Frr. 1 A ii 9; 4, 13; 5 i 11, 13; 5 ii 7).

A commentary, even when well preserved, is not apt to afford much information about the structure of the composition to which it relates, and this is not well preserved. As far as I see all that is to be learned from it is a few more fragments of the text of the *Μαρικᾶϲ* and perhaps that the chorus was divided in a way similar to that of the *Lysistrata*. It may be observed that the name *Μαρικᾶϲ* does not occur. When Hyperbolus is referred to, it is by his proper name (Frr. 1 B iii 5, 1 C ii 7, 12).

Like many commentaries this is written in fairly wide columns. The last line of a note may end within the column but only one full-length line survives complete as written, Fr. 1 B ii 9 of 36 letters. Others can be counted with reasonable closeness, Frr. 1 A ii 9, 1 C ii 6 of 33, Frr. 1 A i 17, 1 B ii 8 of 33 counting the 'filler', 1 B ii 12 of 36, 1 B ii 20 of 38 not counting one which projects into the left-hand margin. But the figures by themselves are deceptive, as the copyist uses blank spaces and enlarged letters (as well as 'fillers') to justify his lines (e.g. Fr. 1 A i 1, 20, Fr. 4, 6).

The lemmas are indicated by a *diple obelismene* above the line in which they begin and a slight projection of the first letter into the left-hand margin. They are usually separated by a blank space from the comment. In one or two places a paragraphus appears to indicate a subdivision within the comment.

The writing, which varies in size from place to place, is of a common type, datable in the second half of the second or first half of the third century. A different hand has made a few corrections. Whether the sparse marginal additions are due to either of these pens or even whether they are all from one, I cannot tell. The title, which is written rather cursively in a watery ink across the top of Fr. 1A, I suppose to have been added subsequently in the third or even the fourth century.

Fr. 1 A

Col. i (a)　　　(b)　　　　　　　　　　　Col. ii

```
      ]. ηκατα[              ]αχειαν·〉[
      ].α..γα[               ]νικαϲενικα· [
     ]τατ[]..αρτ.[           ]καϲενικα            [                  ].α[
     ]υϲ[]....[              ]ε̣νταυτ᾽εϲτ᾽                       καιτ̣αιϲε̣.[
5    ].νεβρον[               ]εωνοϲταυτα                        τουϲπερϲαϲ[
     ]....πα.[               ].με.αι·                           παρεδεξαντ̣[
                                              a
     ]μαϲπαλι̣[              ].ματαυποτροπ[[ι]]ζει               γαραυτοιϲ επι̣[
                                                              ⟩—
     ]υποτροπα[             ]ε̣ι̣ρονδιατιθεαϲιν      [          ] ζητωνγαρω[
     ]. ερχομε[             ]καταλαμβανουϲιν                  ] ουδενκενον[
10   ]..[]μεν̣α[            ].[].αυτοντ[.]ο                   ] ευρεϲτουτων[
    ]ο̣.[ ].[]π̣.[].δ̣[]ηϲθενηκυ[   ]νυνπαλιν                 ]τοιϲαγαθοιϲτ[
    ]φηϲ[.]καταπ[.]ν̣ειϲθαιϲυ[    ]βηϲε[                     ]κενοντρυπη[
    ]υπολλουχρο[.]ονκαιτο.[       ].φε.[                     .].δεμιακε[
    ].τι.[.]παμπ̣[.]υν·[]ηδεμ[    ]φ[                        .]αϲαιλεγειδε.[
                                                              i·
15  [[ραμματοδιδ[.]ϲκαλων.[                                  .].ριτμηματα[
     ].τι]]ηδεμ[..]αφορααπ[...]νγρα̣[                        δερματωνη[
    ]λων πολυνχρονοναφειϲθε 〉                                τωνπεριτεμ[
      ]ϲ̣υγουναλλ᾽εξαλειφετετουτοδ᾽〉                         τοιγαρανθρω[
      ]ν εϲτ̣ι̣ν·λεαινεταϲδελτουϲ·〉                          κολλητεο[
                                                              ⟩—
20      ]ν[  ]ονουτωφθεγξεται ε [                            ετεροϲδε[
         ].τοτεδημειζονφθε̣.ομ̣α̣ι̣.[                        κακω.[
                                                              ⟩—
         ].τοιϲεϲχατοιϲενη[                                  αλλεν[  ].[
         ]κηκαιτοιϲεϲχατ̣[                                   ϲωμεναυτη.[
      ] [   ]  [ ] [                                         ποιηϲωμεν.[
25    ].τεδ[ ]οπρο̣[ ].ντ[                                    ].τελευτα[
     ]προϲφ[ ].ντε[  ]ονδ[                                   ]διδοντεϲτ.[
     ]μειϲκ[ ]νον[  ] [                                      ] ριανικ[].[
    ]ετον.᾽ι.[.]..οπο[  ]ημα[                                ] καιθεοϲ[
    ]αποτουτουολοϲοχοροϲλεγει.[                              ] προϲφερο[
                                                              ⟩—
30  ]ωτεωϲκαινυντοτεωϲαντι[                      ]           οιατ᾽εϲθ᾽ α[
      ]  [ ] [] [          ]                       ]         τοτοιουτο.[
```

]ω.[	]απαcιτοιcκ[	]	δευτερον[
]ουc.[	].ταηδ′με[	]	ι.[].νοι....[
]ιcθ.[	]·εν.[	]	ανανθρωπο[

ζη ⊸

35

]	τιτοκακον ουκ[
]	τουτολεγει μ[
]	α[ ]ρουcλ.[
]	ροντοωcαντι[

⊸

]	αλλῶταμενμ[

40

]	παρατηνπαρ[
]	δημοc αυτημε.[

Fr. 1 A Col. i The left-hand upper part of (a) is rubbed in places, so that the ink has nearly or quite disappeared and the verification of proposed readings will often not be possible.

On the back of this part, in a medium-sized cursive, is ευπο[|μαρικα[

The interval between (a) and (b) is fixed both by the vertical fibres and by the internal evidence in l. 12

1]., traces compatible with μ, if one letter   2]., the lower parts of two uprights; perhaps π, but possibly two letters   Between α and γ, level with the top of the letters, a small crutch (e.g. the central part of the top of τ), followed after a stripped place by a faint dot   3 Before αρ what now looks like γ preceded by a short horizontal stroke having at its left-hand end the tip of an upright. This combination leaves an unfilled space after τ. I am inclined to think it is better to posit ταρ and interpret the tip of the upright as representing the right-hand stroke of η (or the ι of a diphthong) .[, a dot off the line   Of]κ only the end of the lower branch   4]..., the remaining ink could be combined as ων, but these letters would be larger than expected and the ν anomalous. I can make no plausible combination to give three (or four) ordinary letters   .[, a heavy dot, level with the top of the letters   5]., traces compatible with ν or ω   6]....., scattered traces, of which the first might represent ω and the last pair οι   .[, the lower part of a stroke rising to right   ]., the right-hand end of a horizontal stroke coming from left and touching the left-hand stroke of μ; perhaps ε likeliest   Between ε and α the lower part of an upright descending below the line   7]., the upper part of an upright with a trace to right of its top   8]ει, only a trace of the turn-up of ε and the foot of ι   9]., on the underlayer, a trace level with the top of the letters and below it a dot on the line   10]..[, the lower part of an upright, followed by the upper part of an upright Of α[only the extreme left-hand end of the loop   ].[, the top of a circle with a projection at its left-hand end   ]., the tops of two strokes, the first very faint, compatible with ν, but possibly separate letters   Of τ[only the left-hand end of the cross-stroke. Above the following letter or letters (below νc in the preceding line) two parallel horizontal strokes   11 After]ο perhaps ν, but λ followed by an upright may be preferable   Before []π a dot off the line, after π the foot of an upright, followed at an interval by a trace off the line   Of δ[only the left-hand angle   Of]η only the right-hand part   13 Of ολ only the lower left-hand arc of ο and the upper end of the left-hand stroke of λ .[, the lower part of a stroke rising to right   ]., the right-hand stroke of α or λ   .[, an upright, followed by a dot off the line; perhaps two letters   14]., the foot of a slightly forward-sloping stroke   .[, an upright descending well below the line, the tail turning out to left   Of]π only the lower parts of the upright, which appear to have been reinforced in the same way as those of μ next but one following   ]ν has a short upright through its left-hand branch   Of]φ[only the top of the upright 15 .[, a dot below the line   21]., two dots, one above the other, the upper just above the top of the letters   Between ϛ and ο only room for one letter, represented by a dot level with the top of the

letters   .[, a heavy dot with a stroke to right, level with the top of the letters; not prima facie ·7
22]., the top of a stroke above the general level   25]., an upright   Of ọ[only the upper left-hand arc   ]., a trace to left of the left-hand apex of ν   Of τ only the lower part of the stalk, but recommended by the spacing   26]., a dot about mid-letter   Of]ọ only a short piece of the right-hand arc   28 Above ν traces   Between ν and ι only a couple of faint dots level with the top of the letters   After ι the lower part of an upright, followed by traces compatible with the diagonal and upper part of the right-hand upright of ν   [].., two vertically related dots, perhaps representing the foot of an upright, followed by a broad ν or by α (or λ) ι   29 .[, an upright   32 .[, the lower part of an upright   33 .[, a corrected letter? Now resembles κ but not the κ of this hand   ]., a convex upright with foot hooked to right; perhaps ν, though there is now no sign of the diagonal   34 θ damaged; β may be possible. It is followed by a convex upright   .[, the upper part of a slightly forward-sloping stroke

Fr. 1 A Col. ii 3]., the right-hand part of a cross-stroke as of γ   4 .[, the lower left-hand arc of a circle   9 seq. Eupol. fr. 354   13]., a dot slightly above the general level   14 .[, the left-hand end of a cross-stroke as of τ   15]., a dot slightly above the general level   21 .[, an upright   22].[, the lower end of an upright descending below the line   23 .[, an upright   24 .[, a short forward-sloping stroke above the general level   25]., a dot on the line   26 .[, the upper left-hand arc of a small circle   27].[, the upper part of an upright with a trace to left, perhaps of a preceding letter   31 .[, an upright   33 .[, three dots, on separate fibres, in a more or less vertical line   ]., the top of an upright, slightly above the general level   After ι apparently δ, but perhaps α, then the lower part of an upright with a trace to right of its top, followed by the foot of an upright with a trace to right of its top, next δ, or possibly α, followed by what may be the lower left-hand central part of ω   37 .[, perhaps the lower part of the loop of α or of the back of ε   41 .[, on a detached fragment, perhaps not correctly replaced, a dot on the line followed by the lower part of a stroke descending in a flat curve to right

Fr. 1 A Col. i The entry on the back is presumably to be supplemented Εὐπό[λιδοc | Μαρικᾶ[| [ὑπ(όμνημα).

2 seq. When words or phrases recur in the same neighbourhood there is a presumption that the first occurrence is from the lemma, the repetition from the comment. Cf. ll. 7 seq., 13∼17, 20 seq., 22 seq., 25 seq., col. ii 9∼12, 15∼17, 23 seq., 1 B ii 4 seqq., 7 seq., 12 seq., 16∼18, 20∼23 seqq., 1 C ii 8 seq.

Here]νικας ἐνίκα, and the rest of l. 2 to the left, will be a lemma. Possibly an iambic tetrameter, i.e., -νῑκᾱc. . . .

7 Lemma; iambic tetrameter?

ὑποτροπάζει the originally written -ιζει is an unattested form. -αζ- is supported by non-literary evidence of the third century B.C., by some MSS. (e.g. of Phrynich. *P.S.*, Phot. *Lex.*, Pollux) and, if the metre is rightly identified, conclusively by this quotation. -ιαζ- appears to be offered by the tradition of Hippocrates and of Philo, but I have not pursued it further.

The verse may have run something like ἐφ' ἥ-]μᾶc πάλι[ν ‿—].μαθ' ὑποτροπάζει.

8 seq. ὑποτροπ(ι)άζειν is generally intransitive, usually of the illness, 'recur', sometimes of the sufferer, 'relapse'. In this place χ]εῖρον διατιθέαcιν, and perhaps ἐπα]νερχόμενοι (or -αι, sc. νόcοι) καταλαμβάνουcιν, seem to imply a transitive ὑποτροπάζουcι. If this is not delusive, ἐφ' must be removed from the suggested supplement. (For ἐπανερχ- cf. Pollux iii 107 ἐπανῆλθε τὸ νόcημα, ὑπετροπ(ι)αcε τὸ νόcημα.)

11 ἠcθενηκυ[ῖα or some case of it. (The compound διηcθ- cannot be ruled out.)

12 Perhaps φηc[ι].

καταπ[ο]νεῖcθαι cυ[μ]βήcε[ται, -cθαι.

13 seq. The context indicates πολύ]ν in the lemma; for πολὺν πολλοῦ χρόνον cf. Aristoph. *Eq.* 822 πολλοῦ δὲ πολύν με χρόνον καὶ νῦν ἐλελήθηc ἐγκρυφιάζων, *Nub.* 915 (in reference to which Suidas has πολλοῦ ἀντὶ τοῦ πανύ), *Ran.* 1046, al. Eupolis himself has another example of this use of πολλοῦ in the *Βάπται* (fr. 74).

τογ[seems the most likely interpretation of the ink, and then τόν[δ' can hardly be avoided.

].φε.[ἀφεῖcθε indicated by πολὺν χρόνον ἀφεῖcθε, l. 17. The reconstructed lemma is then compatible with an iambic tetrameter.

πάμπολυν would be expected, as an explanation of πολὺν πολλοῦ, and to be preceded by ἀντὶ τοῦ, but I can by no means reconcile the ink after τι—ἀ]ντὶ is acceptable—with τ and ολ would be rather crushed.

14 seqq. [[ἡ δὲ μ[ετα]φ[ορὰ | ἀπὸ τῶν γ]ραμματοδιδ[α]cκάλων .[|].τι]] ἡ δὲ μ[ετ]αφορὰ ἀπ[ὸ τῶ]ν γρα[μ|ματοδιδαcκά]λων: ἡ μεταφορὰ ἀπὸ . . . a regular formula in commentaries, e.g. scholl. Aristoph. *Av.* 450, 462, al., Pind. *Ol.* i 14, Soph. *O.T.* 17.

I can make no guess at the 'metaphor from schoolmasters' seen by the commentator in πολὺν χρόνον ἀφεῖcθε, whether this last word is middle or passive. The next lemma contains words that schoolmasters no doubt used, but as the text stands, the statement about metaphor does not refer to them.

18 seq. ἀλλ' perhaps implies μὴ] cὺ γοῦν.

ἐξαλείφειν is to wash out ink, λεαίνειν to remove writing on wax. [LSJ in v. has no instance of this use of 'smoothe'.]

I see no explanation of the plural in the one case, the singular in the other. The first seems to get some support from ἀφεῖcθε, the second from cὺ γοῦν. There seems to be no possibility of escaping the inconsistency by a different articulation.

20 seq. There is presumably some relation between φθέγξεται and φθε.ομαι, but only one letter (γ or ξ) can be inserted between ε and ο, and I see no explanation of the difference of person.

25 seq. There is a reasonable likelihood that a repetition of προcφέροντεc or πρόcφορόν τε or something of the sort is to be recognized.

27 ἡ- or ὑ]μεῖc and κ[αι]νόν[or κ[οι]νόν[?

29 τὸ]ἀπὸ τούτου or the like. This seems to imply that the two heterogeneous halves of the chorus (v. not. Fr. 1 B ii 18 seqq.) had different parts in what preceded. Cf. Aristoph. *Lysistr.* 1042 ἀλλὰ κοινῆι (old men and women) ξυcταλέντεc τοῦ μέλουc ἀρξώμεθα.

30]ω τέωc a succession also found at Eupolis fr. 117 (from an anonymous play, but assigned to the Δῆμοι).

καὶ νῦν, 'in this passage', τὸ τέωc ἀντὶ [τοῦ πρότερον, πρὸ τοῦ, μέχρι τινόc, simm., cf. scholl. Aristoph. *Thesmoph.* 449, *Nub.* 66, schol. Plat. *Hipparch.* 229 D, et al.

32 κ[ριταῖc is suggested by Professor Fraenkel, who compares Aristoph. *Av.* 445 ἅπαcι νικᾶν τοῖc κριταῖc, Amphis ἐν 'Ιαλέμωι, καὶ τοῖc cοφοῖc κριταῖc ἅπαcιν.

33 ἡ (δὲ) με[ταφορά?

Col. ii 8 seqq. ζητῶν γὰρ ω[.

οὐδὲν κενὸν [τρύπημ' ⟨ἂν⟩ ἐν ταῖc οἰκίαιc ἂν | εὗρεc. At Aristoph. *Eccles.* 624 τρύπημα κενόν occurs *sens. obsc.* In l. 13 ο]ὐδεμία κε[νή may have accompanied a reference to the more or less synonymous τρήμη or τρύμη; cf. *Et. Mag.* 726, 53.

15 seqq. A little, but very little, light is shed on this entry by Hesych. in κόλλεα (out of the correct order; ? κόλλαια): περιτμήματα δερμάτων, ἀφ' ὧν ἕψεται ἡ κόλλα (followed by the jumble τοῦ βυόc, κόλλα τοῦ βοὸc τὸ νωτιαῖον δέρμα ἐξ οὗ τὸ κολλᾶν).

17 των περιτεμ[νομένων.

35 τί τὸ κακόν; 'what the devil?' as at Aristoph. *Pax* 322, *Av.* 1213, *Thesmoph.* 610, fr. 607.

38 Since ἀντί suggests the possibility of ἀντὶ τοῦ, attention may be directed to the articulation -ρον τὸ ὡc, ὡc being a matter for explanation at *Av.* 91 ὡc ἀνδρεῖοc εἶ, where the schol. has ὡc· πολύ. ἐν εἰρωνείαι δὲ τὸ ὡc.

39 seqq. παρὰ τὴν παρ[οιμίαν seems probable, as commonly in the Aristophanes scholia (e.g. *Av.* 507, *Pax* 1078, *Lys.* 68). I can supply no proverb concerning ears, but the presence of δημοc makes it worth while to call attention to the quotation from the Πόλειc of Eupolis (fr. 213), in which there appears to be a reference to a quasi-proverbial expression, 'having wax in the ears' (i.e. thick-headed), in connexion with one Demus, son of Pyrilampes, well known as a handsome young man from mentions in Aristophanes and Plato.

Professor Fraenkel makes what I suppose is a more likely suggestion, that Μ[ίδα should be recognized, comparing Aristoph. *Plut.* 287 and the scholiast there.

Fr. 1 B

Col. i (Col. ii)   Col. ii (Col. iii)

```
      ]˙/.   κυδωνταδ᾽ουκυ[              ]ωνλεγεται
      ]      τωναπαρνουμεν[             ]πειδανε
      ]      λευθεροιγενων[             ]
             >—
      ]   /  εξα..καιπρωιρ[             ].ναντιπρω
 5    ]      ρο̣υ̣τηνγλωττα[             ].αζεπροστο
      ]      λεγειν πρωιραγ.[   ].[   ].αζουλεγεται·
             >—
      ]   ˙/.  καιταισοικιαισα[   ]ειρηκ̣[ ]σεκεινου
      ]        τασοικιας επιτω[   ].ταισοικο̣υντων7
      ]        ουτοσεπιτωνοικοδομηματωναυτοτεθεικεν
        ζη     >—
10    ]   .   φεριδωτιαλκμεων̣[   ]προθυρεπωφε^λ[[λια]]
      ]   ˙/.  ευγενηστισουτος[   ]ων·
               >—
      ]        ειδωσεφοιωνρημα̣τ[   ]ι̣στιγματων·πα.[
      ]        ρηγματαλεγειτ̣[...]υ̣[[περ]][ ]ι̣σποσι οριβατουντες
      ]        γαρκοπτουσιξυλαεστιν[   ]παραμε̣ν̣ανδρωι7
15    ]        τοτοιουτον              [  ]
               >—
      ]        τουτοεκδανιζεικαικυκας[ ].ναυτικονα[        ]
      ]        επιτωιπεμπτωι μερε[   ]τουστοκ̣[              ]
      ]   ˙/.  ναυτικοι·ημεισδαρ οικ[   ]ενοτων
                              c
      ]        πλουσι̣ωνλεγειχο̣ρο[[ν]][
               >—
20   ]c  ζη  καιγαραιγυναικ[.]ςοσαιμ[   ]νεανιαισξυνωσ[  ]
     ]·        καταγελωνται [        ].[]κ̣αιδουλοισιν̣[ ]
     ].        φελουνται·[].[        ]ς̣ι̣ς̣υ̣ν̣[ ]
     ].η·      νεανισκο[                               ]
      ] [      ]δουλο[                               ]
25            ]ο̣νη[                                ]c
                                                   ]
                                                   ]
                                                   ].
```

    ·   ·   ·   ·

It seems to me very probable that what I have designated 1 B contains the remains of the columns immediately following what is contained in 1 A. I cannot follow the fibres with any confidence across the presumed gap, but I believe there is enough agreement to justify the location of 1 B i 20 seq. opposite 1 A ii 18 seq.

There was a 'joint' about the middle of col. ii, clearly visible in l. 9 and just visible in l. 13.

Fr. 1 в

Col. iii (Col. iv)

καιοιμενπενητε[
οιδεπλουσιοιτωδες[
κοινωcοτιεντοιc[
>—
ουτοcτικεκυφαc.[
5 .[]βολον λεγειτοημιχορι[
 >[]
λακεδαιμονιουcμεν.[
ταc· αποκοινουτ[.]υλε.[
>—
απολωγαραυτουc·ω.[
.υπροcχωρουνταcπ..[..]..[
10 ζη δυεινταττεταιτ[.]..[].υμν[
  ]·τοεν.[].ουc...[
παραγεινεcθαιδεδ[
ουcεφημαc.[ ]α.[
νηδιαδεδοι[
15 γεμετουτε[
μεινπρ[
δεπελθο.[
κωcιν ει[
κλεωνπαφλ[
20 παφλαζειν[
 >—
ωcπεργενη[

 δ
 ω κωc ενικαα[
 οιχοροιοταν[
·/.
 αλλοτριοιcπ[
25 πον cτρατη[
ελομεν cτ[
]εcτρατηγη[
]ξαcαλλα[
].ταλλα[
30].οπλ[
 >—
 ]εγ.[

 . . . .

Fr. 1 B Col. i 20 ζη, though close to the column on its right and far from that on its left, must presumably refer to the latter. The same remark is presumably true of the ζη between Col. ii ll. 9 seq., above, although in this case it would have been possible to suppose that Alcmeon was to be the subject of 'inquiry', if the ζη relevant to this line had not survived close to Fr. 1 B iii 10   22]., perhaps the upper part of ε with an elongated cross-stroke   23].η, the tops of two strokes, perhaps representing a small ν. If a note, peculiarly placed in relation to the high stop

    Col. ii 4 Between α and κ a trace level with the top of the letters, followed by a dot about mid-letter   ]., a trace at the bottom of the first upright of ν; perhaps α   5 Of ϝτ only the lower ends of the diagonal and second upright, and the extreme ends of the foot of the stalk and right-hand part of the cross-stroke   ]., the lower part of an upright   6 ι anomalous   .[, the start of a stroke rising to right   ].[, a dot on the line   ]., the middle part of a slightly convex upright   7 Of κ[only the middle part   8]., the lower end of an upright descending below the line   10 Above δ something written, which looks like a small χ; not casual ink   12 Of τ[only elements of the lower end of the stalk   .[, the top and the lower end of an upright descending below the line 16]., the upper end of an upright   21].[, a dot level with the top of the letters   22].[, the same   Of]ϛιϛ only the tops   25]ϲ is noticeably further to right than any of the preceding line-ends   28]., the top of an upright. This is below the last letter of l. 25, that is, exceptionally far to right

    Col. iii 4 .[, a loop on the line, open to right   5 In the margin a horizontal stroke not quite level with the top of the letters and having traces above and below its right-hand end   6 .[, a dot below the line   7 .[, a convex stroke   8 .[, a slightly forward-sloping sinuous upright 9 Before ν apparently ρ, but the fibres are disordered   Of π only the first upright and the foot of the second; after this only dispersed traces of the feet of letters on a frayed-out strip   10 After τ[.] traces of the feet of letters on a frayed-out strip   Before ν apparently the top right-hand arc of a small circle   11 All up to the stop has vanished with the over-layer   .[]. a dot about mid-letter, followed after a gap by a fainter and slightly lower dot   ...[, the lower part of an upright, followed by traces on a single fibre of the tops of two or three letters; the last may combine with a clearly preserved upright to form ν   13 .[, a horizontal stroke a little below the level of the top of the letters   α.[, the upper left-hand arc of a circle   14 Of διαδ only the tops   15 seq. In the left-hand margin a monogram like an elongated ρ with a thick ν across its tail   17 .[, a slightly forward-sloping upright   26 Of τ[only the left-hand part of the cross-stroke   29]., the upper part of an upright   30]., the extreme right-hand end of a cross-stroke level with the top of the letters   31 Of χ only the angle, but π less likely   .[, a short cross-stroke level with the top of the letters

    Fr. 1 B Col. ii 1 seqq. κυδῶντα κυδάω is not recorded. The comment presumably says, 'it is a word used of'—what? To go by ἐ]πειδὰν ἐ]λεύθεροι γένων[ται, of slaves who deny that they have been slaves, say, ἐπὶ δούλ]ων . . . τῶν ἀπαρνουμέν[ων δούλων γεγονέναι. But this may not be the only possible reconstruction, and it does not enable a precise interpretation of κυδᾶν to be arrived at.

    4 seqq. ἔξαγε can be accepted, but is not verifiable. It might be intransitive.

    The article of Hesychius, πρωιράσαντεϲ· κροτήϲαντεϲ. ἡ δὲ μεταφορὰ ἀπὸ τῶν νεῶν καὶ τῆϲ εἰρεϲίαϲ, makes reasonable the assumption of an otherwise unattested πρωράω. [LSJ deduce πρωράζω. I do not see on what grounds.] An imperative πρώιρα gets some support in this place from the imperative ἔξαγε preceding and what look like imperatives -αζε, -αζου following.

    The meaning would appear to be more or less similar to that of ῥοθίαζε, which may be recognizable in l. 5. This is explained as 'row hard', e.g. by Hesych. in ῥοθιάζειν, Phot. in ῥόθιον, Eustath. 1540, with reference to Aristoph. Eq. 546. (If it occurs in Eupol. fr. 324, it is in a different use.)

    But ἀντίπρωρον seems to imply the presence somewhere of πρῶιρα rather than πρώιρα. ἀντίπρωρον τὴν γλῶτταν metaphorically, 'tongue ready for action against the enemy'?

    If ῥοθ]ίαζε πρὸϲ τὸ λέγειν, I suppose 'press on to say' is likelier than 'press on is put with reference to saying', exemplifying a frequent use of πρόϲ in the Aristophanes scholia.

    I suppose it is likely that].αζε and].αζου are endings of the same verb. The alternative hypothesis that].αζου is the ending of a noun, πρῶιρα γὰρ ἐπὶ (or ἀντὶ) -.αζου λέγεται, is excluded by the absence of any noun in -αζοϲ (or -αζηϲ) which could be considered remotely probable. But if πρώιρα γὰρ ἀντὶ τοῦ ῥοθιάζου is assumed—and it seems to square, at least partially, with what is assumed at the beginning—it seems necessary, in spite of the methodological objection involved, to emend to ῥοθίαζε, since a middle of ῥοθιάζειν is neither attested nor expected.

7 seqq. εἰρηκ[ότο]c ἐκείνου τὰc οἰκίαc ἐπὶ τῶ[ν ἐν α]ὐταῖc οἰκούντων οὗτοc ἐπὶ τῶν οἰκοδομημάτων αὐτὸ τέθεικεν. An example of the first, οἰκίαι for 'families', in Eupolis himself at fr. 117, 5 (probably Δῆμοι). But what is meant by ἐκείνου? The clause οὗτοc—τέθεικεν by itself would, I think, certainly be taken as 'our author uses the word οἰκίαι in the sense of buildings', but no contrasted person is apparent, of whom ἐκείνου would be a sufficient specification. The only alternative I see is to understand ἐκεῖνοc and οὗτοc as characters in the play, the second of whom takes wrongly the sense of a word used by the first. But I can adduce no parallel for τιθέναι meaning 'take as' as opposed to 'employ as'. In commentator's language that would normally be (ὑπο)νοεῖν or ἀκούειν.

10 seq. The correction presumably denotes ἐπωφελ(εῖ).

From the comment that this Alcmeon was εὐγενήc τιc I suppose it may be inferred that he was not a legendary hero, whether the son of Amphiaraus or the son of Sillus. Which, if any, of the other recorded bearers of the name he was, and what, if anything, he had to do with πρόθυρα, I cannot guess. The line looks as if it may have resembled Aristoph. *Nub.* 648 τί δέ μ' ὠφελήcουc' οἱ ῥυθμοὶ πρὸc τἄλφιτα;

For the form of the note cf. schol. Aristoph. *Av.* 798 Διτρέφηc· οὗτοc πολυπράγμων.

12 seqq. I suppose ῥη⟨γ⟩μάτων is intended. ῥήγματα and cτίγματα are different kinds of wound, 'lacerations' (Hesych. in ῥῆγμα· ... κατὰ μῆκοc τραύματοc οὐλή) and 'punctures' (cf. schol. Aristoph. *Vesp;* 1296 cτιζόμενοc ἀντὶ τοῦ κεντούμενοc).

παρ[ὰ τὰ | ῥήγματα λέγει τ(ὰ) ὑπ(ὸ) [το]ῖc ποcί. I can offer no parallel to τ̈ for τά (though it is found in use for other cases of the article) nor to ῦ (which simply repeats the corrected ὑπέρ) for ὑπό.

13 seq. I cannot determine the bearing of this apparently inconsequent remark. I find nothing of the sort in the Menander that has survived.

16 seqq. τοῦτ' ἐκδαν⟨ε⟩ίζει καὶ κυκᾶ⟨ι⟩c [τὸ]ν ναυτικὸν α[: the final α is awkward, but though it is damaged I can see no other letter as likely, and ᾰ[◡ − ◡ is not irreconcilable with an iambic tetrameter, which the noun wanting after τὸν ναυτικόν would be apt to produce.

τὸν ναυτικὸν α[: 'the shipping accounts'? τοὺc τόκ[ουc and ναυτικοί suggest that some matter of bottomry is in question. (τ)ὸ ναυτικόν, 'the fleet', was not written.)

ἐπὶ τῶι πέμπτωι μέρε[ι: 'in the fifth act'? I should have expected, in this sense, κατὰ τὸ π. μέροc, cf. **2257** fr. 1, 8, but M. Aur. *Med.* xi 1 has ἐπὶ παντὸc μέρουc and the dative would not be essentially different. On the other hand, δανείζεcθαι ἐπί with a dative of the rate of interest or the security is regular usage.

18 seqq. ἡμεῖc δ' ἄρ' οικ[   ]εν· ὁ τῶν πλουcίων λέγει χορόc. ἡμεῖc κτλ. evidently a lemma, and since it does not start at the beginning of the line, perhaps the continuation of the preceding lemma which does so. Professor Fraenkel suggests οἴκ[αδ' ἄπιμ]εν, comparing Aristoph. *Vesp.* 255, *Av.* 1636.

The chorus seems to have consisted of a mixture of πένητεc and πλούcιοι (v. col. iii 1 seq.), so that χορόc here apparently might have been ἡμιχόριον, cf. col. iii 5, fr. 5 i 12. Aristophanes' *Lysistrata* similarly has a non-homogeneous chorus, partly men, partly women.

20 seqq. Lemma iambic tetrameters:

καὶ γὰρ αἱ γυναῖκ[ε]c
ὅcαι μ[ὲν ἂν] νεανίαιc ξυνῶc[ι | καταγελῶνται,
ὅcαι δὲ   ].[]καὶ δούλοιcιν | ὠφελοῦνται

cυνεῖναι is neutral, but here there can be no doubt to be taken *in malam partem*. This may also hold of ὠφελοῦνται, though I find no example of such a use, on comparison with ἐπικουρία as employed by Aristophanes at *Lysistr.* 110. δούλοιcιν may then be governed by ξυνῶcι. It need hardly be said that it cannot stand for ὑπό (παρά, πρόc, simm.) δούλων.

Col. iii 2 τῶι δεc[πότηι cf. Fr. 1 C 7.

4 seq. οὗτοc, τί κέκυφαc; Aristophanes has οὗτοc, τί κύπτειc; *Eq.* 1354, *Thesmoph.* 930, but I do not think that a difference in the persistence of the position is implied. At *Lysistr.* 1003 and *Nub.* 191 the perfect is used.

At the end perhaps πρὸc τὸν Ὑπέρ]|βολον λέγει τὸ ἡμιχόρι[ον.

6 Λακεδαιμονίουc μεν.[, perhaps as far as -]|ταc, l. 7, lemma.

7 ἀπὸ κοινοῦ, as a technical expression, 'applying to both (or all) of two (or more) words or clauses', cf., e.g., schol. Theoc. viii 58.

9 seq. ἐπὶ]‖ δυεῖν τάττεται? 'is used of two things', 'has two uses', cf., e.g., Ap. Dysc. π. ἀντ. 84. 7, schol. Plat. *Phaedo* 60 B.

12 seq. Λακεδαιμονί]ουϲ?

14 I suppose νὴ Δία δεδοικ[is likely to be from the play, though it is not apparently part of the lemma.

19 seq. I should guess something like Κλέων Παφλαγὼν λέγεται παρὰ τὸ παφλάζειν (ἀπὸ μεταφορᾶϲ τοῦ παφλάζειν); cf. schol. Aristoph. *Eq.* 919, Eustath. 360, 28, al.

καὶ ἐν τῶι Μαρικᾶι (as well as the revised Νεφέλαι) προτετελεύτηκε Κλέων schol. Aristoph. *Nub.* 552.

22 ω⁸ can, prima facie, be nothing but ᾠδή, which must refer to the text on its right. In that case, it would be expected to be written opposite l. 21, not between ll. 22 and 23. But I do not think that a commentary would be expected to have a reference of this kind in the margin at all. If a technical division of the comedy was to be alluded to, it should be in the commentary itself. Moreover, if Fr. I C ii is the continuation of this column, there is no sign that it is in fact an ᾠδή. I can offer no solution of this problem.

26 ελομεν is surprising and I cannot account for it.

Fr. 1 c

Col. i (1 B Col. ii) (Col. iii)   Col. ii (1 B Col. iii) (Col. iv)

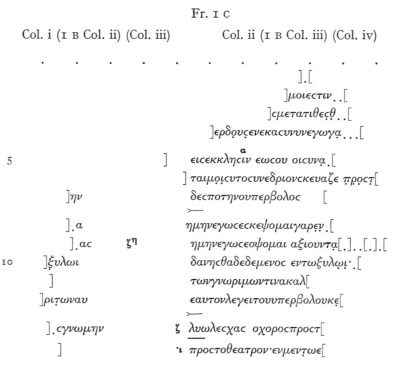

I am fairly confident, though I cannot establish the fact by means of either the horizontal or the vertical fibres, that these are the lower parts of the columns of which the upper parts are Fr. 1 B Col. ii (Col. iii), Col. iii (Col. iv). If so, the piece can be located fairly closely on the basis of the following considerations. The number of lines in the column deducible from Fr. 1 A is 41. If there was the same number in this case, the first four lines of the lower piece must be right-hand parts of the last four lines of the upper. There cannot have been fewer than 41; it is not very likely that there were more than one or two more.

Fr. 1 c Col. i 8]., a dot on the line   9]., a dot level with the top of the letters   13].,
elements of an upright descending below the line

Col. ii 1 The end of an upright below the line   2 ..[, parts of a triangular letter, followed by
a trace on a single fibre   3 To left of]c traces of about six letters on frayed-out and twisted
fibres   Of ϛθ only the top and bottom; after this perhaps αι but only traces on a single fibre
4 ...[, traces on a single fibre   5 .[, the lower end of an upright below the line   6 Of τ[
only the left-hand end of the cross-stroke   9 Of α[only the bottom left-hand angle   ]..[, the
overhang of ε suggested, followed by a short horizontal stroke level with the top of the letters   ].[,
the upper end of a stroke descending to right; perhaps represents a triangular letter   10 Of ωι
only the tips   .[, a dot level with the top of the letters   13 seq. Against the beginning of the
first of these lines is a large ζ, of the second letters which might be interpreted in more than one way;
ωι appears to be likeliest

Fr. 1 c 4 κ]έρδους ἕνεκα, unless an error for εἵνεκα (as, e.g., Aristoph. *Thesmoph.* 360), part of the
comment.

4 seqq. cύ νυν· ἐγὼ γὰρ ..[| εἰς ἐκκληcίαν· prima facie words of the play.

εἰς ἐκκληcίαν regularly without article, e.g. Aristoph. *Ach.* 28, *Eccles.* 270, 289, 352, 490, *Eq.* 936.

ἕως οὖ οἱ cυνα.[-ν]|ταί μοι, cὺ τὸ cυνέδριον cκεύαζε. πρὸc τ[ὸν | δεcπότην ὁ Ὑπέρβολοc. cὺ — cκεύαζε
presumably gives the sense of the sentence cut off by the parenthesis.

'You get the meeting together' cf. Plat. *Protag.* 317 D βούλεcθε οὖν . . . cυνέδριον καταcκευάcωμεν;

8 seqq. I do not see how to avoid the conclusion that ὄψομαι is offered as an interpretation of
cκέψομαι. But it must be remarked that cκέψομαι 'inspect' finds a rather rough-and-ready equivalent
in ὄψομαι and that the position of γάρ as sixth word is even more extraordinary than in Aristoph. *Lys.*
489 διὰ τἀργύριον πολεμοῦμεν γάρ;

γὰρ ἐν .[Since ἐν ξύλωι may be suggested I am bound to say that the remains of the last letter,
minimal though they are, do not look to me compatible with the base of ξ, which they would have to
be taken to represent.

9 ...]‖ δ' ἂν ἦcθα δεδεμένοc ἐν τῶι ξύλωι   δῆcαι, δεδέcθαι ἐν (τῶι) ξύλωι v. Blaydes's collections app.
crit. ad Aristoph. *Eq.* 367.

11 seq. τῶν γνωρίμων τινὰ Καλ[| ἑαυτὸν λέγει?

13 λύω λέcχαc: Πλάτων φηcὶ λέγεται ὁπόταν ἐπὶ τὰ ἔργα ἐξήρχοντο (Plat. com. fr. 223). 'We must get
to work' 'The chorus addresses the audience'?

If ζ|ωι is rightly read, Ζωί(λοc) is presumably indicated, but I do not know what it would signify.

14 πρὸc τὸ θέατρον cf. Aristoph. *Ach.* 629 οὔπω παρέβη πρὸc τὸ θέατρον λέξων . . ., *Pax* 735 αὐτὸν
ἐπήινει πρὸc τὸ θέατρον παραβάc . . ., *Eq.* 508 λέξονταc ἔπη πρὸc τὸ θέατρον παραβῆναι.

It may be worth while to remark that at this point the commentary may have reached the parabasis; both the lemma λύω λέcχαc and, if it is a lemma, πρὸc τὸ θέατρον are compatible with the anapaests to be expected and are suitable in content.

Fr. 2

```
          ·      ·       ·
            ].c[
            ]ν[
            ]ω[
            ]..[
  5         ]ντ.[
            ]αρεικ[
            ]ην[
            ]ν.[
            ]η[
          ·      ·      ·
```

Fr. 2 Perhaps from fr. 1 A i in the neighbourhood of the right-hand side of the left-hand part of ll. 32 seqq.

1]., elements of an upright   4 Two traces off the line, followed by a forward-sloping upright stroke with a faint trace to right about mid-letter   5 .[, an upright   8 .[, the lower part of an upright

Fr. 3

```
          ·     ·      ·
            ].ιτη[
            ]μιc[
          ·     ·      ·
```

Fr. 3 Perhaps from the lower part of fr. 1 A i

1]., the right-hand end of a cross-stroke level with the top of the letters

Fr. 4

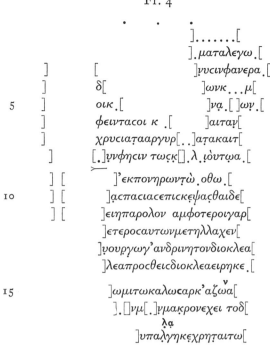

Fr. 4 1 Faint and dispersed traces;]αιδιδωμ[appears acceptable, but only the last two letters can be said to be likelier than any other interpretation of the ink   2]., the right-hand end of a cross-stroke as of γ   .[, the edge of an upright?   3 .[, a dot below the tail of α (which is itself anomalous)   4 Below and to left of δ a trace of a stroke descending to right   Between κ and μ the surface is nearly destroyed; τη seems possible   5 .[, a dot on the line   After ạ the lower part of an upright   .[, a dot on the line   6 κ is abnormally large and has a blank space on either side   .[, the top of an upright   8]., prima facie the underside of the loop and the lower part of the right-hand stroke of α; no letter would be lost between this and κ   Between λ and ἰ perhaps the tip of an upright   Of ω only the base of the right-hand part   .[, the lower parts of two uprights; perhaps two letters represented   9 Of τ only the extreme left-hand end of the cross-stroke and the bottom of the stalk   After ὡ traces compatible with the top and bottom of the first upright of ν   .[, γ or τ or possibly π   13 Eupol. fr. 433   Between γ and ω what looks like a small apostrophe; apparently without significance   14 .[, a trace level with the top of the letters and another below and to right   15 c made out of γ   16].[, a trace level with the top of the letters   κ by alteration? It has on it a number of apparently meaningless strokes   τοδ[by a dif·ferent hand?

Fr. 4 There is ink opposite the beginnings of ll. 4 seq. which presumably belongs to the preceding column.

5 γυ]ναι[κ]ων.[may be possible.

7 τὰ] χρυcία τὰ ἀργυρώματα, 'gold ornaments, silver plate'. Perhaps cf. Eupol. fr. 155 (Κόλακεc) ἀρπάζουcιν ἐκ τῆc οἰκίαc τὸ χρυcίον, τἀργύρια πορθεῖται.

8 I suppose, ν]ῦν φηcιν 'the dramatist says here', but [ο]ὖν φηcιν is another possibility.

Since some ingenious person may think of τω⟨ι⟩ Cκ[ε]λλίου τω⟨ι⟩ Αρι[cτοκρατει or τωι Καλλιυυ τωα.(.)[I may as well say that I think neither can have been written.

9 seq. Presumably τῶι νόθωι in reference to Pericles' son by Aspasia. Cf. Eupol. fr. 98 (Δῆμοι), al.

10 seq. I should expect the sense to be: ἐπισκέψασθαι δεῖ πότερον Ξάνθιππον λέ|γει ἢ Πάραλον. ἀμφότεροι γὰρ γνήσιοι. . . . Cf. Plut. Pericl. 24, 8. But the first is too long in this form.

12 ἕτερος αὐτῶν μετήλλαχεν. (I should have expected μετηλλάχειν; perhaps some such alternative as μετηλλαχέν[αι λέγεται should be preferred.) In fact *both* of Pericles' sons by his first wife died within a few days in the plague 430/29 B.C. For though Plut. Pericl. 36, 6 has ἀπέθανε γὰρ ὁ Ξάνθιππος ἐν τῶι λοιμῶι νοσήσας, in Consol. Apoll. p. 118 E we find Περικλέα δὲ . . . πυθόμενον ἀμφοτέρους αὐτοῦ τοὺς υἱοὺς μετηλλαχέναι τὸν βίον, Πάραλόν τε καὶ Ξάνθιππον . . . .

13 Lemma. οἰς]υουργῶι γ᾽ ἀνδρί, 'a maker of wicker-work' (baskets, hurdles, etc.).

νὴ τὸν Διοκλέα. At Aristoph. Acharn. 774 this oath is put in the mouth of a Megarian and explained by the scholiast by reference to a Megarian hero also mentioned by Theocritus (xii 27 seqq. See Gow's note on l. 29). It does not look as if such an explanation would be relevant here. I suspect that all that was said was that the very common νὴ τὸν Δία was converted by the 'addition' of κλεα into Διοκλέα. But προσθείς is not a very precise way of describing the change and I see no point in it, unless indeed wicker-work was a Megarian speciality.

15 Lemma? . . . δίδ]ωμι τῶι καλῶι.

σαρκάζων seems to have given trouble. I suppose it is part of the exposition, not of the lemma: the poet speaks 'mockingly'. Cf. schol. Aristoph. Av. 1009 ἐν σαρκασμῶι φησιν (more commonly ἐν εἰρωνείαι, e.g. ibid. 91, 135, 798).

17 ὑπαλλαγῆι κέχρηται τῶι . . . 'by a transference the poet has used the word *x* in place of the word *y*'.

Fr. 5

(a) Col. i   Col. ii

. . .   . . .

```
                                        ] προστοδιδο.[
                                        ] κορινθιων.α[
                                        >
        ].[                             ] οστισπροδοσιας τ[
     ]σκος[..].[                        ] κληθησομαι εισδικ[            (b)
     ]και.ω              5              αγοραων τωνκατα[          . . .
     ].τιμην                       ✕    προτελουσι προπη[            ][
5    ]                                  >
     ]τινων·                            φουσιναυτοκαβδα[          ]δαλα[
     ]ιλευς                        ✕    λεγεταιταεπικαθ.[         ]ιωθασι[
                                        καπτειν αιαλετρι[         ]εκ[
     ]α..ονλακεδαι       10        >    φατνισματαδε τα[          ]ομε[
     ]                                  ναφρυ.[                   ]..[
10   ]μηνειστα                          τρεφους[
     ]ξυνηλικες                         θαρτοι[                   . . .
     ].οντοημι        [                 ]μη.τ.[
     ]ρωφρενοβλα      [                 ]—
     ]            [
15   ]....[.....]...με.[
```

. . .   . . .

Fr. 5 Col. i 1 On the line a loop open upwards   2]., if one letter, ν, but perhaps α or λ followed by the foot of an upright   3 Of ι only the foot, followed by a dot and a horizontal stroke on the line   4]., an upright; ν suggested   8 After α the lower parts of two uprights descending below the line   11 Eupol. fr. 181, 5   12]., two dots slightly below the level of the top of the letters   τọ might be taken for γθ   13 Eupol. fr. 181, 7   ]ρ apparently corrected or remade   15]....[, the tops of letters, the first represented by a horizontal stroke, the second by the top of an upright (ι?), the third by a loop (ο or ρ?), the fourth by a dot   ]..., the tops of letters, the first suggesting ε, the second δ or λ, the third ο or ρ   .[, two dots, one above the other, the lower off the line

Col. ii 1 .[, the start of a stroke rising to right   2 Between ν and α the edge of an upright 4 The first κ has apparently been converted into β, but the resulting letter is anomalous. The paragraphus below it is by a different pen from the rest   7 Eupol. fr. 200   8 .[, a dot on the line 10 The mark above φ perhaps meant for a paragraphus. Possibly by the same hand as that below l. 4   11 .[, a loop on the line open to right; α, or possibly δ, suggested   (b)]..[, the top of a thick upright, followed by the top left-hand part of a circle   14 η anomalous; the remains perhaps wrongly combined   Before τ the top of a small circle, after τ a trace attached to its crossstroke

Fr. 5 Col. i 11, 13 seq. The ends of the verses ἠκούcατ', ὦ ξυνήλικεc and ὑμεῖc γάρ, ὦ φρενοβλαβεῖc, which form part of Plutarch's quotation from the Μαρικᾶc intended to illustrate his account of Nicias' character (*Nic.* 4). But I see nothing in the preceding which looks as if it could have any relevance to the other part of Plutarch's quotation.

12 seq. Possibly τὸ ἡμιχόριον.

Col. ii 3 seq. ὅcτιc προδοcίαc and κληθήcομαι (or δια]βληθήcομαι?) both appear to be parts of a lemma. Professor Fraenkel suggests τ[ήμερον | κληθήcομαι, which looks attractive.

The point of Plutarch's quotation (Col. i 11 seqq.) is a frivolous accusation against Nicias of treachery, but more than half a column separates the two mentions of treachery in this commentary.

5 ἀγοράων presumably part of a quotation from an epic poem. The form occurs once in the *Iliad* (ii 275), once in the *Odyssey* (iv 818), not in Hesiod. (Δι]αγοράων, 'of atheists', is a theoretical possibility, but why should this have had an epic form?)

6 Only three verbs are recorded beginning with προπη-. None have any recognizable relevance to προτελοῦcι in any acceptation. Nor can I suggest any, if the articulation πρὸ πη- is chosen.

7 The *diple obelismene* implies that this line is a lemma. No other lemma, as far as I can tell, begins, as this must, in the line before the *diple.* Another anomaly is that the φ, so far from projecting slightly to left, starts (on the same alignment as the following lines) indented slightly to right.

7 seqq. On the basis of Hesych. αὐτοκάβδαλα· αὐτοcχέδια ποιήματα εὐτελῆ it is a reasonable guess that φουcιν may represent γράφουcιν. Some light is thrown on the comment by the Lycophron scholia (*Alex.* 745) κυρίωc...ἡ λέξιc ἐπὶ τῶν ἀλφίτων εἴρηται. τὰ γὰρ ὡc ἔτυχε φυραθέντα ἄλευρα αὐτοκάβδαλα (cf. *Et. Mag.* 173, 53), but not enough to enable me to offer a plausible suggestion about τὰ ἐπικαθα-, though I suppose some form or derivative of καθαρόc lurks there. ἅπερ εἰώθαcι κάπτειν αἱ ἀλετρίδεc might apply to lumps in badly made dough, but I suspect that this clause has been appended for the sake of the etymology, not for its factual truth, especially since ἀλετρίδεc might be expected to grind corn, not to make dough.

9 seqq. The strict sense of ἐκφατνίcματα is τὰ ἐκβαλλόμενα ὅτε καθαίρωcι τὰc φάτναc Hesych. In a slightly extended use it is applied to crumbs that fall from the table as at Athen. 270 d and, metaphorically, at Philostr. *v. Apollon.* i 19. Here I should suppose that it was applied contemptuously, 'sweepings', to the products, whatever they were, already qualified as 'botched' (αὐτοκάβδαλον . . . τὸ εἰκῆ καὶ ὡc αὔτωc καὶ αὐτουργὸν γεγονόc schol. *Alex.* 745, *Et. Mag.* 173, 52). [Pollux x 166 has ἐκφατνίcματα δὲ αἱ cανίδεc αἱ ἀναιρούμεναι ἐκ τῆc φάτνηc ὡc καθαίρεcθαι τὰ περιττά. If this is true, it has no obvious applicability here.]

11 φρυα-, which is unavoidable—no known Greek word begins φρυδ-—suggests nothing else as likely as φρύαγμα or some cognate, but the connotation of these is not 'empty noise' but 'overbearing behaviour'.

Fr. 6

Col. i   Col. ii

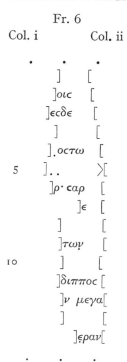

Fr. 6 4]., perhaps the right-hand part of the loop and the bottom of the stalk of ρ   5].., the upper part of an upright, followed by what may be meant for ο, though angular and flattened 6 ϲ made out of γ, apparently by the original hand   12 Above ν the original hand wrote ω; the same or another thickened the side-strokes of this and placed a diagonal between them, projecting below the foot of the right-hand one. The result resembles a roughly made ν, but I do not see what purpose this would have had

Fr. 6 6 ϲαρ, as at fr. 4, 15, made out of γαρ and perhaps, as there, a form or derivative of ϲαρκάζω. 11 Possibly Ποϲεί]διπποϲ, like Menander, who is referred to at Fr. 1 B ii 14, a writer of the New Comedy.

Fr. 7

Col. i   Col. ii

```
         ·    ·        ·    ·      ·
    ]υ.[.]..[
    ]           [
    ].η.ιγωνια[
    ].αρ[.].c[.]ντε        [].[
5   ]                      cυ[
    ].υπαρα..              ⁄[]υποτ[
    ]..ηρκεcται·           προ[
    ]μαρ.[]..[]            .[.].[
      ]ι.υο[  ]ι           φ.[
10        ]υρ             το[
          ].              []..[
         ·    ·        ·    ·      ·
```

Fr. 7 Col. i 1 .[, the start of a stroke rising to right   ]..[, the lower part of an upright below the line, followed by a dot on the line   3]., an upright   After η apparently ν, but possibly μ   Of γ only the foot of the stalk (to right of which a faint dot not accounted for) and the right-hand end of the cross-stroke   4]., κ or χ   Before c the upper part of an upright   6]., an upright; η perhaps suggested   .., a dot below the line, followed by a dot on the line   7].., the top of an upright, followed by the upper part of an upright with traces to right of its top   Of η only the looped top of the right-hand upright   8 .[, below the line the start of a stroke rising to right; might be taken for an 'acute' on ο, l. 9   ].., above the tops of the letters the top of a stroke rising from left, followed by the top of a small circle   9 Between ι and υ a rubbed δ or possibly α; not c   11]., two dots, possibly the ends of the branches of υ, but the second may be a stop

Col. ii 4].[, a dot, apparently below the line   5 Below this line a *diple obelismene* might be expected, but though there is damage I do not think a *diple* could have disappeared without trace   8 .[, the foot of an upright below the line   ].[, the upper part of an upright   9 .[, ε or θ   11 Tops of letters (perhaps even three, if τ was the first) which I cannot articulate

Fr. 8

```
       ·    ·      ·
    ].ο.[
    ].ωντα[.]χαιρ.[
    ]ειν·παρατοαρχι.[
       ]κοιcιν...[
5      ].ποκα.[
       ].ν[
         ·    ·    ·
```

Fr. 8 1]., the lower end of an upright below the line   .[, a headless upright descending below the line   2]., κ or χ, but a cross-stroke through the lower branch not accounted for   .[, the middle part of a slightly convex upright   3 .[, a triangular letter   4 ...[, perhaps the end of the loop of α, followed by the tip of an upright, and this by the left-hand angle of γ or π or possibly ϲ   5]., perhaps the upper right-hand curve of the loop of ρ   .[, the lower part of an upright 6 Of υ only the tips of the arms; preceded by a speck at a slightly lower level

Fr. 8 3 παρὰ τὸ Ἀρχιλ[όχου or -λ[όχειον, cf., e.g., scholl. Aristoph. *Av.* 250, 1240. A reminiscence of Archilochus in Eupol. fr. 357.

Fr. 9

```
    •      •      •
]. .[.]. τ[
]εγνω[
].   [
    •      •      •
```

Fr. 10

```
         •      •
]...[
       ⌐
]   η[
]   .[
]   τα̣[
       ⌐
5   ]   μ[
[stripped]
]   ϲτρ[
[[⌐]]
]   α̣ει[
       ⌐
]   ε̣πε[
10  ]   ο[
       ⌐
]   ϲ[
]   δε̣[
       ⌐
    •      •      •
```

Fr. 10 1]...[, the foot of an upright; the lower part of a circle with a projection from the top right-hand end, perhaps θ; the foot of an upright   3 .[, the foot of an upright   4 Above α an interlinear dot

Fr. 11

$$].\!.\omega\lambda.[$$
$$]\nu\epsilon\mathsf{c}..[$$
$$]...\delta\omega[$$
$$]o\nu\ \alpha\iota\mu..[$$
$$5\qquad]\mathsf{c}\ o.[$$

Fr. 11 1]..., a dot off the line, followed by the turn-up of a stroke on the line   .[, perhaps the upper part of ε, but on a twisted projection   2 ..[, the start of a stroke rising to right with two dots above, followed by a dot on the line   3]..., two uprights with foot hooked to right, followed by ι or υ   Of ω[only the left-hand stroke   4 ..[, a dot about mid-letter, followed by a trace level with the top of the letters   5 .[, the lower part of an upright

Fr. 12

$$].[]\epsilon[$$
$$].[].[$$
$$].\iota\tau\eta.[$$
$$]\alpha\tau\eta\gamma o\mathsf{c}\ o\upsilon[$$
$$5\qquad].[]\epsilon.\upsilon\tau\omega\iota[$$
$$]\tau\eta[\ ]\ [$$
$$]o\lambda\eta\kappa o.[$$
$$]\epsilon\nu\ \alpha\pi\rho o\mathsf{c}[$$
$$].[.]\delta\alpha\nu\iota\zeta\omega[$$
$$10\qquad]\rho\tau\eta\kappa o\tau[$$
$$]\eta\mu\epsilon\iota\mathsf{c}[$$
$$]\omega\nu\ o[$$
$$]\ [$$

Fr. 12 1 seq. Rubbed   1]., the foot of an upright   2 Hooks open to right on the line 3]., an upright   η anomalously large   .[, the apex of a triangular letter?   4 Of]α only the end of the tail   5].[, the base of a small circle   After ε the apex of δ rather than of α suggested 7 .[, apparently τ or υ, but either anomalous   9].[, perhaps υ, but possibly the lower end of a stroke descending from left and the lower part of a slightly forward-sloping upright   12 The col. ends in this or the next line

2742. Commentary on an Old Comedy

The following fragments, to judge by the only one large enough to warrant an opinion, come from a commentary on Old Comedy. It displays some learning, but there are apparent in the text a number of faults, some minor (ll. 11, 19, 23), one at least major (ll. 12 seq.), and perhaps others (ll. 20, 21, 22), about which I am uncertain. As to the play commented on, I offer the guess that it was the Cερίφιοι of Cratinus. Perseus and Polydectes are mentioned in a lemma, and though I have said that I do not see how Perseus can be taken in that place as a person in the action except after emendation, it is obvious that the first nineteen lines imply the participation of a character who spent a greater or shorter time suspended in the air, as Perseus does in the Cερίφιοι (Cratin. fr. 207, 1). A slight corroboration of Cratinus' authorship is afforded by Hephaestion's singling him out as handling paroemiacs as they are handled in ll. 19 seqq. It should perhaps be added that, except for the Δανάη of Sannyrio, no Old Comedy but the Cερίφιοι has a title from which a play relating to the story of Perseus can be deduced.

The articulation of the commentary which it must be supposed was intended has not been very accurately executed. The *diple obelismene* stands correctly under ll. 19 and 27 in each of which a lemma starts; it has no meaning under l. 26. A blank space is left before the beginning of a lemma in l. 30, but not in ll. 19 and 27; after the end of a lemma in ll. 28 and 32, but not in l. 22. There are other blanks, of which that in l. 13 may have been left to accommodate a correction, but that in l. 26 has no purpose. The end of each of the three quotations is marked with a high stop, ll. 11, 16, 19.

The writer of this manuscript is the same as that of **2306** (Alcaeus commentary) and **2368** (Bacchylides commentary).

Fr. 1

. . . .

```
          ]..[                        ]..[
         ]ειρης[                     ]ειρης[
    ]τ[.].ραδοπα.[              τ[.].ραδοπα.[            ἔ-
      ]λεγονδουτω[             λεγον δ' οὕτω[
  5   ]μακρανεξης[             μακρὰν ἐξ ἧς [
    ].ενουσανω[      ]ελε [    μένους ἀνω[      ]ελε-
    ..]νπροσδε..[.].ομεγων  [  ]ν προσδες.[.].ομένων.
        ]αττισαταλ[..]τωιαποτης [  ͻτρ]άττις Ἀταλ[άν]τωι· ἀπὸ τῆς
   ]  κραδησεηδηγαρισχασγι.[   κράδης· ἤδη γὰρ ἰσχὰς γίν[ομαι·
 10  ]  ομηχανοποιοσμωσταχιστα [ ὁ μηχανοποιός μ' ὡς τάχιστα
     ]  καθελετω· ενφονισσαις [ καθελέτω. ⟨καὶ⟩ ἐν Φο⟨ι⟩νίσσαις·
     ]  διονυσοσοσθυρσοισιναυληται [ Διόνυσος ὃς θύρσοισιν αὐληταὶ
     ]δεΙ·Λ κω[...].νεχομαιδιε [ δεΙ·Λ κω[...].ἐνέχομαι δι' ἑ-
     ]τερωνμοχθ[..]ιανηκωκρε [ τέρων μοχθ[ηρ]ίαν ἥκω κρε-
 15  ]μαμενοσωσπερϊσχασεπικρα[  μάμενος ὥσπερ ἰσχὰς ἐπὶ κρά-
     ]δης·αριστοφανησγηρυταδηι[ δης. Ἀριστοφάνης Γηρυτάδηι·
     ]  περιαγεινεχρηντονμηχα[  περιάγειν ἔχρην τὸν μηχα-
     ]  νοποιονωσταχιστατηνκρ[  νοποιὸν ὡς τάχιστα τὴν  κρά-
     ]  διην·ουτωδητονπολυδεκ[ δ{ι}ην. οὕτω δὴ τὸν Πολυδέκ[την
          ⌐
 20  ]  βαλλειστοισσκωμμασινειε.[ βάλλεις τοῖς σκώμμασινειε.[
     ]  περσευσκαιτουποδοσελκεις[ Περσεὺς καὶ τοῦ ποδὸς ἕλκεις
     ]  καιτησυπερασιναρκιηστ.[  καὶ τῆς ὑπέρας, ἵν' ἄκρ' ἵηις. το[ῦ
     ]  ποδοσελκειοιονευρυθμω.[  ποδὸς ἕλκει⟨ς⟩ οἷον εὐρύθμως
     ]  τιθειστονποδαωσανειαντι[  τιθεὶς τὸν πόδα, ὡσανεὶ ἄντι-
 25  ]  κρυσεφηκαιτουρυθμουελκ.[  κρυς ἔφη· καὶ τοῦ ῥυθμοῦ ἕλκε[ις,
     ]ει.θ.εξης  ηυπεραιψυχℙωσπρος [ εἶθ' ἑξῆς ἡ ὑπέρα ψυχρῶς πρὸς
     ]τονποδαγνωσειμεντοικα    [ τὸν πόδα. γνώσει μέντοι κα-
     ]τατωνπτερνων εναφιης    [ τὰ τῶν πτερνῶν  ἐναφίης
     ]κατατωνσκελωνμεχριτων   [ κατὰ τῶν σκελῶν μέχρι τῶν
 30  .].[.]..].ων  αλλαχορευτης [ π]τε[ρ]νῶν. ἀλλὰ χορευτὴς
        ].πανυστατοσαιειπλην  [ ].πανύστατος αἰεὶ πλὴν
        ].νον επειδηεις       [ ].νον ἐπειδὴ εἰς
                      λι
        ]ετασμο[[νο]]σεφοιτων [ ]ετας μόλις ἐφοίτων
        ]νηρωσοθε.[     ].[    ]νηρως οθε.[      ].[
 35      ].[]νη[                ]ωνη[
```

. . . .

Fr. 1 3 To left of τ[, slightly higher than the cross-stroke, a sign like a shallow 'short' with a tail at its right-hand end   ]., on the line a hook to right   .[, the lower part of an upright descending below the line; ρ acceptable   4 εγ ετ could be read   7 .[, the start of a stroke rising to right above which the upper end of a stroke descending to right   ]., flat on the line the end of a stroke from left   10 Ink not accounted for to right of last α   13 Of]ε only the lower curve   20 .[, off the line the lower left-hand arc of a circle, below which a short horizontal stroke hooked under at its left-hand end   31]., the edge of a low upright   τ the natural decipherment is ιτ and perhaps I should not have rejected it   32]., a very short median upright, followed by a dot on the line   34 .[, a dot at the end of the cross-stroke of ε

Fr. 1 4 seqq. I have indicated what I suppose to be the likeliest articulations, but there are other obvious possibilities in each line.

It may be inferred from the quotations in ll. 8–19 that above l. 8 there was a lemma containing a mention of the κράδη. I cannot recognize elements of it in the remains, but ll. 5 seqq. may be plausibly interpreted as part of a description of the use of a sort of crane.

ll. 5 seq. E.g. ἀρτω-, αἰωρου-μένους.

8 There are references to a play of Strattis variously named Ἀτάλαντος (schol. Aristoph. *Ran.* 146, Suid. in cκῶρ ἀείνων), Ἀταλάντη (Athen. 302 d, 399 d, *vit. Isoc.* p. 256 W.), and even Ἀταλάνται (Suid. in διφροφόροι). Though this is a far from fault-free manuscript, its confirmation of Ἀτάλαντος I should say confers finality on the argument that the error of Ἀταλάντη for Ἀτάλαντος is many times more likely than the converse. Νίοβος and Νιόβη are similarly confused in references to Aristophanes' play Δράματα ἢ Νίοβος.

8 seq. ἀπὸ τῆς κράδης. Pollux iv 128 ὃ δ' ἐcτὶν ἐν τραγωιδίαι μηχανή, τοῦτο καλοῦcιν ἐν κωμωιδίαι κράδην. δῆλον δ' ὅτι cυκῆς ἐcτι μίμηcιc. κράδην γὰρ τὴν cυκῆν καλοῦcιν Ἀττικοί. Cf. [Plut.] παροιμ. ii 16 κράδηc ῥαγείcηc· κράδη νῦν οὐχ ὁ cύκινος κλάδος ἀλλ' ἡ ἀγκυρίς, ἀφ' ἧς οἱ ὑποκρίται ἐν ταῖc τραγικαῖc cκήναιc ἐξαρτῶνται. Simm. Hesych. in κράδη.

9 I have hung till I'm shrivelled.

10 ὁ μηχανοποιός the operator, Aristoph. *Pax* 17, *Daedalus* (fr. 188).

12 Διόνυcοc ὃc θύρcοιcι the first words of the *Hypsipyle* of Euripides, schol. Aristoph. *Ran.* 1211.

12 seqq. As a god Dionysus might say ἥκω κρεμάμενος κτλ., but I cannot guess at the construction or relevance of the intervening words.

In regard to the letters at the beginning of l. 13 it had occurred to me that the copyist's exemplar may have been damaged so that Ι·Λ was all that he could make out of ΚΑ. At all events κακοῖc, or κακῶc preceded by some other dative, ἐνέχομαι is an acceptable phrase in the context.

19 seqq. Paroemiacs, used consecutively as here by Cratinus; Heph. *Ench.* viii 6 Κρατῖνοc ἐν Ὀδυccεῦcι cυνεχῶc αὐτῶι (sc. τῶι παροιμιακῶι) ἐχρήcατο.

I can contribute little to the understanding of the lemma or the comment.

τὸν Πολυδέκτην βάλλειc . . . Περcεύc can, I suppose, mean nothing but 'you are a Perseus pelting Polydectes . . .', that is to say, a character in the play is compared to Perseus, who is therefore not a character in the play. But the legendary Perseus did not throw anything at Polydectes. If the correct reading was Περcεῦ, then Perseus (and with him Polydectes) would be a character in the play, no doubt the air-borne character whose presence is implied in the passages adduced above. But I can make nothing of the word at the end of l. 20.

τοῦ ποδὸc ἕλκειc primarily means nothing but 'you drag by the foot'. But the continuation καὶ τῆς ὑπέρας transforms ποδόc into a rope. I can find no evidence that τοῦ ποδὸc καὶ τῆc ὑπέρας ἕλκειc could be said for 'you haul on the sheet and the brace'.

The commentator's contribution (or contributions, for I do not see how 'you place the πούc εὐρύθμωc' is plainly equivalent to 'you drag by the ῥυθμόc'), may import a third stratum of witticism based on the relation of 'rhythm' to '(metrical) foot'. I do not see how he extracts this from the text.

(From the scholia on *Od.* v 260 it appears that ancient commentators were not agreed about the ropes to which the names πούc and ὑπέρα apply.)

ιvακριηc if there is no error, I can articulate only as I have, but I can come to no conclusion about the meaning. 'In order to let go ends.' ἄκρα occurs as a noun referring to part of a ship in Alc. 34, but apart from any other consideration a noun in this kind of writing requires the article.

27 seqq. 'Down over (your) heels' means 'down over (your) shanks as far as (your) heels', or,

since 'you' are performing the action (e.g. of spilling), for '(your)' some other person may be due to be substituted.

(I may remark, though I do not think it can be relevant, that πτέρνη was the name of part of the mast of a ship, Eratosthenes ἐν τῶι Ἀρχιτεκτονικῶι ap. schol. Ap. Rhod. *Argon.* i 566.)

31 seq. Presumably to be divided . . . αἰεί | πλὴν . . . .

Fr. 2

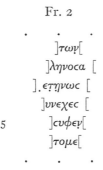

Fr. 2 The cross-fibres appear to fix this scrap on a level with Fr. 1, 28–33. If I am not mistaken in locating it to right, it belongs presumably to the next column.

1 ρ[, the top of the left-hand side   3]., a speck on the line. The letters are rubbed; for τη I am not sure that γει might not be read, though ε is not now easy to accept

Fr. 3

Fr. 3 1 In greyer ink and at less than the normal distance from the next line a flat stroke on the line and the lower part of a stroke curving down from left through its right-hand end. There is also

above its left-hand end what looks like the beginning of a horizontal stroke level with the top of the letters   5 .[, an upright through the tail of *α*; e.g. an inserted *ι*   11 .[, a speck on the line
12 .[, a speck level with the top of the letters

Fr. 4

.   .   .
] ταδευ‚ε παρ.[
] οτιοποτεμελλ[
] αζεϲθαιανεχω[
]προ.[].[   ]·[
.   .   .

Fr. 4 1 Of *υ* only the left-hand branch. Between it and *ε* the lower part of an upright descending well below the line   .[, perhaps *α*, but the fibres are displaced   2 *ε* is quite unlike the normal *ε* and cannot be said to be *deciphered*   4 .[, perhaps the upper end of a stroke descending to right
].[, a horizontal stroke level with the top of the letters

2743. STRATTIS, *Λημνομέδα* (AND OTHER PLAYS?)

The attribution to Strattis of the following fragments is dependent on the identification of fr. 1, 7 with a quotation from his *Λημνομέδα* (Strattis fr. 23), but as the quotation is a proverb, the identification is less than certain, since proverbs are apt to be repeated in more than one place. I have recognized no other line from this or any other play of Strattis. Even if the identification is correct nothing is revealed about the meaning of the title and next to nothing about the contents of the play. I have not had much success in combining the fragments, and the variations in the writing may show that they were in fact spread over a wide area, though the difference between adjacent columns in fr. 8 is a warning that this argument cannot be pressed. The only piece sufficiently continuous and metrically uniform to offer reasonable prospects of interpretation is fr. 8 ii 1–10 and my failure to make much of this does not encourage me to make more than strictly limited contributions on less well-preserved pieces of mixed metrical constitution such as fr. 1, fr. 8 i, fr. 11.

An error at fr. 1, 15 has been corrected. Another at fr. 8 ii 2 is uncorrected, and, if the last word of fr. 8 i 13 is erroneous, that too is uncorrected.

The hand, which varies noticeably in size between the extremes frr. 22–23 and frr. 24–27, is an upright, rounded book-hand of a common type to be dated in the second century. In some pieces the uprights have separately added serifs at the foot, in others the serifs are replaced by a hook or may be omitted.

Fr. 1

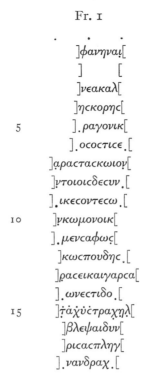

```
            ·     ·     ·
        ]φανηναι[
        ]         [
        ]νεακαλ[
        ]ησκορης[
  5     ].ραγονικ[
        ].οcοcτιcε.[
        ]αραcταcκωιογ[
        ]ντοιοιcδεcυν.[
        ].ικεcοντεcω.[
 10     ]νκωμονοικ[
        ].μενcαφως[
        ]κωcπουδης.[
        ]ραcεικαιγαρcα[
        ].ωνεcτιδο.[
 15     ]ταχὺἐτραχηλ[
        ]βλεψαιδυν[
        ]ριcαcπληγ[
        ].νανδραχ.[
```

Fr. 1 5]., the right-hand end of a cross-stroke touching the top of ρ   6]., a speck on the line with a hook to its right on the line; perhaps λ   .[, the left-hand ends of strokes compatible with ξ and perhaps ζ   7 Strattis fr. 23   8 .[, the left-hand end of a cross-stroke, as of τ   9]., the lower end of a stroke descending with a curve from left   11]., the right-hand arc of a circle   12 .[, a dot below the line   14]., a trace of a cross-stroke, as of γ   .[, the left-hand ends of rising and falling strokes; perhaps λ or χ   18]., prima facie ο, but ω acceptable .[, the left-hand arc of a circle

Fr. 1 7 Schol. Plat. *Lys.* 205 Ε λέγεται δέ τις καὶ παροιμία ἀπὸ τούτου . . . ἀφ' οὗ καὶ Cτράττις Λιμνο-πέδαις· Χῖος παραστὰς Κῶιον οὐκ ἐᾶι λέγειν. The name of the play is given as Λιμνομέδων in Suid. Cτράττις, as Λημνομέδα in Athen. 327 e and 473 c, and in Harpocrat. ἁπλᾶς, and this is generally taken as correct.

The line is prima facie an iambic trimeter. I do not see how l. 10 can have been an iambic trimeter, assuming a loss on its left of an amount equivalent to χιοcπα. (In l. 8 τοῖοιcδε is available, as, e.g., Aristoph. *Pax* 1258 ἐὰν τοῖαυτασί κτλ.)

Fr. 2

```
        ]cουνεοικ[
        ]τροφηνεπε[
```

Fr. 2 2 Of]τ only the extreme right-hand end of the cross-stroke

Fr. 3

Col. i   Col. ii

]		.[
]		α[
]		ε[
]		ω[
]	5	αδ[
]		ọ[
]		ς̣[
]		α[
]		.[
]	10	[
]		π[
]		.[
]		[
]		[ ]αν.[
]	15	α..[].[]λα...[
]		δεοϲγαρουκε[
]	κ.	θεωνεκητι.[
]		πληγαϲοκακ[
]		εοικαμεντ.[
]	20	ουγαρλελυϲι̣[
]		τολημαται.[
]		καιτοι̣τ̣ι̣το[
]		νυνδηδαπωλ[
]		ιϲαντιϲωντο[
]	25	εωϲαναντεχ.[
]		αγαθονγαρ[
]		ων[
].αξεν		ψυχ[
		πωϲ[
	30	ϲυγα[

Fr. 3 Col. i]., an upright with a trace on the left-hand side of its foot; ν? The letters, though perhaps written by the same hand as the rest, are much smaller and may be a marginal entry

Col. ii 9 .[, o or c   12 .[, the top left-hand arc of a circle   14 .[, on a single fibre a cross-stroke level with the top of the letters   15 . .[, on the line the bottom left-hand arc of a circle followed by a cusp   ].[a dot on the line   . . .[, two headless uprights rather near one another, followed by a dot on the line; I should guess ιγ .[17 *marg.* after κ a zigzag stroke   .[, an upright with a projection to left at top; π not particularly suggested   19 .[, the lower end of a stroke rising to right; perhaps the underside of the loop of α   21 .[, an upright with a projection to left at top   22 What I have rendered ιτ might be a badly turned out π, but the preceding τ can hardly be c   25 .[, the edge of an upright   26 Below the first letter barely visible traces, presumably of a paragraphus or *diple cum paragrapho*

Fr. 3 At each indention the beginnings of the lines start to slope outwards anew, so that the left-hand edge of the column is a zigzag.

ii 17 The marginal entry, of which I do not know the meaning, looks as if it related to the column on its right.

θεῶν ἔκητι Attic texts in general present ἕκατι. θεῶν ἕκατι e.g. Aristoph. *Lysist.* 306, on which cf. Blaydes's collection.

20 λελυcιτέληκε.

24 ἴc' ἀντ' ἴcων the same expression Plat. *Leg.* vi 774 C.

Fr. 4   Fr. 5

Fr. 4 1] . ., the base of ε or c, followed by the foot of an upright   3] . ., the lower right-hand arc of a circle against ν

Fr. 5 1] . . ., a serif, followed by a short arc of the base of a circle and a speck on the line; I am uncertain how many letters

Fr. 6   Fr. 7

Fr. 6 1] . ., perhaps the right-hand upright of η   2 .[, the upper end of a stroke descending to right

Fr. 7 1] . ., the lower part of an upright touching α   .[, the middle part of an upright or convex stroke with suggestions of a stroke to right at its upper end   2] . ., the end of a turn-up on the line   .[, the start of λ or μ?

Fr. 8

(a)   Col. i   Col. ii

```
                  ]βριζωνε[            ]
                  ].αρδικην [          ]        καιμηναραφυλλοναπορυπουπ...ϲ..[.]ν[
                  ].χωναρηνφρονηϲιν              ϲυδουνδιαχνεπιταιϲπτε[.]ναιϲ...[ ].[
           ]φαιν[.]ταιπαϲινεναργη              ϲεμνονδιακυϲοϲαλευωντηιδ·εμοιδα.[
  5       ]λοκακαιπολυμηχανιδειν               μακροϲγαραγανπεριπορνηϲμ..οϲηγ.[
           ]ομενουδενεχονταπεραι        5      λαμπωναδετονκορακοϲθεωπ[..]...κ[
           ]νγαραπλουντιπεφυκεβροτοιϲ           τιϲουκανορωνπαρατιλαιτενκακοιϲιν.[
           ]τελουμενοιϲινεργοιϲ                 παιδωντερατα ιμε.ατυμπανωντεπ..[
           ]ουμενονουκιϲαϲινουδορωϲιν           πολειϲδεβαρυϲτεναχουϲιχρημα.α[
                                                                     ξ
  10      ]νδεπολινβλεπουϲι                     μιϲθουϲϲυνελεξατοπολλωνρηϲεω[
           ].αϲεχεινολονδεμηδενορθωϲ     10     ωϲτοικοδομεινπαρακαιπαιδων.[
                                                       ⇥
           ]λιανειναινομοντιθενται              πολυωνυμεπλουτεκαιϲυδη[
           ]..αμενοιϲ·τουϲπανταϲεξιουντεϲ       ξενικοϲκορο[c. 7 letters]..[]τυρω.[
           ]εικηχοληνμελα[..]αν                 ολιγον.[ ]...[        ]επειϲαϲ[
  15      ]νηγιανανηκεν                [
           ]νλεγωτον[..]δρα [          ]  15    [
           ]νλωικε.[..]ει  [           ]        [
           ].ρεχειωπρο.[               ]        [
           ]οϲεχων      [              ]       ..[
  20      ]παμπονηρ[                   ]       αλ[      (b)  .    .    (c)  .    .
           ]κομενος [                   ] 20   ϲα[        ]..[           ]πει.[
           ].ροπου  [                   ]      κ.[        ].τα[          ].[[ϲ]]νπ[
           ]τοκεων  [                   ]      λ[         ].ο.[          ].τι.[
           ]..[.].  [                                    ]κη[           ]ηνκ[
  25            ].ωϲπ[                                   ]θυρ[          ].ον[
                ]ρεν[
                ]νημιν[                                   .    .    .    .    .
           ].ελων.[
           ]νεχθρ[
  30      ].γηϲαι[
           ].ετα[

          .    .    .    .    .    .    .    .
```

Fr. 8 (*a*) Col. i 2]., the cross-stroke and the lower end of the stalk of γ or τ   3]., a trace slightly higher than the tops of the letters   9]o written on *a currente calamo*   11]., apparently the right-hand side of a small loop at mid-letter; not ρ   13].., the lower part of an upright, followed at an interval by an upright with a serifed foot, prima facie ι   14 Above κ a stroke like a slightly arched 'acute'   17 .[, a dot on the line   18]. the ends of strokes from left, the upper nearly flat and touching ρ opposite the loop, the lower rising from the line and touching ρ at mid-letter .[, the lower left-hand arc of a circle   22]., an upright; whether π or τ not verifiable   24 Only traces of the extreme tops of letters   25]., an upright, above which a sign like half a large 'circumflex', which I think is used for an apostrophe; cf. fr. 24, 6   28]., the right-hand end of a cross-stroke touching the top of ε .[, the upper left-hand arc of a circle 30]., the edge of the lower part of an upright   31]., a slightly backward sloping upright

Col. ii The right-hand side of ll. 1–8 is rubbed, so that some letters have almost, some have completely vanished.

1 After π perhaps the right-hand stroke of α, followed by a stroke on the line like the base of δ and this by the left-hand side of a circle   After ς the left-hand end of a cross-stroke as of τ with the lower left-hand arc of a circle below, then scattered specks and a blank space up to ν[2 After ς perhaps a shadowy ι and the left-hand parts of π, followed by a short stroke with a thickened right-hand end on the line   3 .[, perhaps the upper left-hand part of λ likeliest   4 Between μ and ο remains compatible with the right-hand arm of ν and the upper left-hand arc of a circle .[, the left-hand side of a circle   5 After π[blank for about two letters, then the upper left-hand part of a circle, followed by short arcs from the top and bottom of a circle and the upper part of an upright having faint traces on left and below to right   6 .[, a dot at mid-letter   7 Between ε and α a speck, nearer α, level with the top of the letters; the spacing suggests τ   Of ς only the top, ο possible, of π the cross-stroke and the top of the left-hand, the top and bottom of the right-hand upright After π perhaps α acceptable, followed by elements of an upright with specks to left and right   8 Of ρ only the top of the loop, of η only the top of the left-hand, the top and bottom of the right-hand upright   Between ᾳ and α perhaps the right-hand side and the right-hand end of the cross-stroke of θ   10 .[, the upper left-hand quarter of ε suggested but θ perhaps possible   12].., the extreme right-hand end of a cross-stroke, as of γ, followed by the extreme top of a stroke descending to right .[, perhaps the start of a stroke rising to right   13 .[, the upper part of an upright ᾳς[, ᾳ might be δ or λ, but there is now no sign of a cross-stroke in ς   18 αθ[or λε[20 The levels of (*b*), (*c*) relatively to (*a*) and to one another are fixed by the cross-fibres. I cannot follow the vertical fibres with enough confidence to fix their intervals, but I believe that (*c*) stands under the right-hand side of (*a*), and that (*b*) stands more or less under ουτ in (*a*) ii 11   20 (*b*)].[, the ink now looks like μ̄, but I think this must be an illusion due to the loss of a cross-fibre and that two, or even three, letters may be represented (e.g.].ςς[)   (*c*) .[. the left-hand arc of a circle   21 .[, the top left-hand arc of a circle   (*c*) Above the cancelled ς what looks like an angular ω   ν and π are run together; π could be interpreted as, e.g., ιτ and perhaps in other ways   22 (*b*)]., what now looks like γ but may be part of π (or even τ?)   .[, a speck level with the top of the letters (*c*)]., a dot level with the top of the letters and a speck below on the line   .[, the left-hand arc of a circle   24 (*c*)]., an upright with foot hooked to right and having traces to right of its top

Fr. 8 Col. i 3 ἔχων ἄρ' ἦν φρόνησιν to judge by the apparent length of the line perhaps an iambic tetrameter.

ἔχων ἦν although analogous periphrases are not uncommon in both verse and prose, the only parallel I can adduce from comedy—but it may itself represent tragic diction—is Aristoph. *Thesm.* 77 εἴτ' ἐστ' ἔτι ζῶν εἴτ' ἀπόλωλ' Εὐριπίδης (*Ran.* 37, *Eccles.* 1094 are of a different nature).

4 φαίν[ε]ται.

5 Perhaps πολύπ]λοκα cf. Aristoph. *Thesm.* 463 πολύπλοκον νόημα, where the lengthening of υ has aroused suspicion. Cratinus is credited with αἱμυλοπλόκος.

6 I suppose οὐδὲν ἔχοντα πέρα is likely to be meant. The spelling πέραι is not uncommon, and, to judge by the fact that ι is sometimes a subsequent addition, e.g. at **1176** fr. 39 iii 16, depends on some doctrine.

7 ἁπλοῦν τι.

13 ἐξῑοῦντεϲ appears to be unmetrical and, as far as I can tell, 'derusting' has no particular relevance. It is easy to elicit metre with a minimum of change, but I can suggest nothing that obviously suits the context.

14 χολὴν μέλα[ιν]αν cf. Menand. *Epitrep.* 560 seq. μελαγχολᾶν several times in Aristophanes; explained as μαίνεϲθαι, v. Aristoph. *Plut.* 903 c. scholl. and Menand. l.c. 558 seq.

16 τὸν [ἄν]δρα.

17 I cannot verify κελεύει. In fact except for a trace on the inside of the curve, which may well be a result of the damage which the surface has suffered, I should opt for κο.

Fr. 8 Col. ii The first ten verses must be presumed to be ◡ – ◡ ◡ – ◡ ◡ – ◡ – ◡ – ◡ – ◡, though this fact is obscured by the loss of all endings—but that of l. 4 may be restored with fair certainty—, a deceptive spelling—in l. 1 απορυπου for απορρυπου—, and a corruption—in l. 2 διαχν in place of an anapaest. As in the ἔξοδοϲ of Aristophanes' *Wasps* there is a cut after the eighth, or the ninth, or the tenth syllable.

1 As this verse contains a complete sentence and (on the above presumption) has not entirely lost more than two syllables, it should be possible to decipher the remains between π and ν[, if one had a clue to the meaning. I have found none.

καὶ μὴν ἄρα is not a collocation of words that I have found elsewhere. I am fairly confident that it is not in Aristophanes.

φύλλον ἀπὸ ῥύπου, whether so articulated or ἀπο⟨ρ⟩ρύπου from a verb found only in Hesych. †ἀπινοῦται ἀπορυποῦται. πίνοϲ γὰρ ὁ ῥύποϲ, suggests no line of interpretation to me. The next letters could be read, though with no certainty, παδοϲ, and since the only recorded Greek noun beginning παδ- is πάδοϲ, a sort of cherry-tree, I mention this possibility on the offchance that the concurrent mention of leaf and tree has some significance.

The theoretical possibility μῆν' ἄρ' ἄφυλλον seems hardly worth notice.

2 †διαχν† Besides the obvious metrical defect there is to be taken into account the possibility of error in δια, which stands almost exactly above δια in l. 3. A second person singular present indicative (or possibly a participle) is expected.

πτέ[ρ]ναιϲι I suppose 'strutting' or the like would be suitable in the context but I can find no evidence that walking 'on the heels' was ever used to describe swaggering.

3 ϲεμνόν adverbial, cf., e.g., ἁβρὸν βαίνουϲα Eur. *Med.* 1164, but the plural seems to be preferred: ϲαῦλα, Anacr. fr. 168, Simon. Amorg. fr. 18, *Hom. h. Herm.* 28, κορωνά Anacr. fr. 151, ἁβρά Eur. *Tro.* 821.

διακυϲοϲαλεύων new; similarly Aristoph. *Vesp.* 1173 ϲαυλοπρωκτιᾶν, explained by the schol. ϲαλεύειν τὸν πρωκτόν. See Blaydes's collections on *Vesp.* 1169.

After τηιδ apparently a high stop. Elision seems to be shown by the sign found at fr. 8 i 25, fr. 24. 6.

4 μῦθοϲ and, I suppose, ἠγο[ρεύθη or ἠγόρευται. The uncompounded aorist and perfect are said not to occur in Attic.

5 Λάμπωνα. No doubt the χρηϲμολόγοϲ who was the butt of Cratinus (frr. 57–58, 117), Aristophanes (*Av.* 521, 988), and, according to Athenaeus (344 e), of Callias and Lysippus.

5 seq. τίϲ οὐκ ἂν ὁρῶν παρατίλαιτο . . . ; 'who would not tear his hair to see—' I suppose, somebody acting in some way. But I cannot choose among the ambiguities of l. 5 an interpretation which looks prima facie probable.

I have considered the possibility of the active παρατίλαι, but (1) I do not know of any evidence that -αι for -ειε is found in Attic writers, (2) τ' would become supererogatory and τον would have to be read for -τ' ἐν. The ε is in a damaged place, but ο cannot be read unless ink has run along a fibre to produce the appearance of a cross-stroke.

7 παίδων τ' ἔραται Aristophanes accuses Lampon of deceitfulness, Cratinus and the other two of gluttony.

μετὰ τυμπάνων probable.

8 seq. 'Cities bitterly lament the moneys which . . . he has collected in payments for his plentiful speeches.'

10 'So he can afford to build . . .', ὥϲτ' οἱ πάρα.

παίδων ἐ[ρᾶν or the like.

Fr. 9

Fr. 10

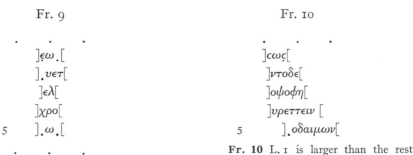

Fr. 9
· · ·
]εω.[
].υετ[
]ελ[
]χρο[
5   ].ω.[
· · ·

Fr. 10
· · ·
]cωс[
]ντοδε[
]οψοφη[
]υρεττειν [
5   ].οδαιμων[

Fr. 9 1 Of]ϵ only the ends of the cross-stroke and the turn-up   .[, the foot of an up-right   2]., prima facie the right-hand side of θ, but the end of the cross-stroke may be illusory   5]., the right-hand end of a cross-stroke touching the top of ω   .[, the left-hand arc of a circle

Fr. 10 L. 1 is larger than the rest   5]., the edge of the lower part of an upright

Fr. 10 4 π]υρέττειν the end of the line.

Fr. 11

· · ·
].αρημωντηνυπρο.[
].cευωχουχαρινδ[
]εντανωcεγωιμαιτημ[
]ονυcοντουτραγουτουτ[
5   ]ιουccκωληκεcειλυπου[
]θοινωcεγαρδικαιονωπρε[
]υχαιcκαλει:πρεπονταcω[
].νκυκλωφερωνοτην.[
]cιχρηταδεπανταμε.[
10   ]ενκαιρω   [
]οιπρωcονεcτεμ[
]δευρι[

· · ·

Fr. 11 1]., the right-hand end of a cross-stroke, as of γ   .[, γ or the left-hand parts of π   2]., a short arc from the upper right-hand side of a circle   3 Of μ[only the base; I do not know that λ followed by a circular letter could be ruled out   8]., traces suggesting the top of a circle   .[, a dot level with the top of the letters   9 .[, an apex, as of δ or λ

Fr. 11 More than one metre appears to be represented in ll. 1–9. Dialogue indicated in l. 7.
3 μ]έντᾶν, ὡς ἐγῶιμαι, τήμ[ερον?
4 Δι]όνυcον.
6 θοινῶ or some other form of θοινᾶcθαι more probable than a compound -θοινοc.
11 πρῶcον cf. Hesych. in πρόcον· ὤθηcον, πρῶcον· ὤθηcον.

Fr. 12

·   ·   ·

].α...[
]πει.[
]ογοι[
]παγ[
5   ]γγελ[
].νι[

·   ·   ·

Fr. 12 1]., a speck level with the top of the letters   After α the foot of a stroke hooked to right, three traces on and near the line, the left-hand end of a horizontal stroke on the line   2 .[a small left-hand arc of a circle level with the top of the letters   6]., the top of a circle

Fr. 13

·   ·   ·

].[
]ογοcε.[
]ωcδοκ[
]μαcπι[
5   ].ακ[
]νταχ.[
].ωτο[
]..ουυ[
]ολουπρ[
10   ]εγειcεπα.[
]εc..β.[
]ουτ.[
].....[

·   ·   ·

Fr. 13 1 The foot of an upright well below the line   2 .[, the edge of an upright   4 ς has a cross-stroke within its upper curve which makes it look like ε, but not quite the ε of this hand, and the ink of the cross-stroke is fainter than the rest   5]., perhaps].γ acceptable, but γ is dwarfish, and this would be true of]τ, the only alternative I see   6 .[, the lower left-hand arc of a circle; ω likelier than ο   7]., the right-hand end of a cross-stroke touching the top of ω   8].., a short arc from the left-hand side of the base of a circle and the right-hand part of a cross-stroke touching the top of ο   10 .[, a slightly concave upright   11 After c apparently no choice but λα, though λ is anomalous and α scarcely retains any sign of the upper side of its loop   12 seq. seem to be rather crushed   12 .[, opposite sides of ο or ω?   13 Tops of letters: of the second the top of a circle; of the third the tip of an upright hooked to left followed by a stroke rising to right, κ suggested; of the fourth the apex of a triangle

Fr. 14

```
        ].ιτε.[
        ]ρπαcα[
        ]νιχον[
        ].ι   [
  5     ]κνιcωι   [
        ]νεcτηι   [
        ].[  ]πι.[
         ].   [
          ].[].[
```

Fr. 14 1]., the lower right-hand arc of a circle   .[, the top of an upright with a trace to right; κ apparently possible   4]., the upper right-hand arc of a circle   7 .[, a sinuous stroke descending from left; the surface between this and ι destroyed   8]., the top and foot of an upright?   Dots near the right-hand edge of the fragment perhaps not parts of letters   9]..[, a stroke level with the top of the letters rising to right in a shallow convex curve, followed at the same level by a short thin stroke rising to right

Fr. 14 3 Proper nouns in -ιχος are plentiful (v. Blaydes on Aristoph. *Ach.* 954) but those in -νιχος are only a small proportion of them. Aristophanes has three, of which I suppose Φρύνιχος is the likeliest to recur in comedy. Φρύνιχος itself has in Aristophanes reference to four different persons (schol. *Ran.* 13; *Av.* 749).

6 Θ]νέcτηι Phrynichus the tragedian does not appear to have written any play in which Thyestes could have been a character.

Fr. 15

```
        ]οιμα[].[
        ]ξυνε..[
        ]τονθ[
        ].[
```

Fr. 15 Beginnings of lines.
1 Of]οι only the lower parts; θ might be an alternative for ο, but I do not think ρ or υ or ι   Of α[only the lower part of the loop   ].[, a stroke rising to right from the line   2 ..[, δ or λ, followed by the upper left-hand corner of ε or θ   4 A short arc from the top of a circle

Fr. 16

```
            ·    ·      ·
            ]εϲτ..[
          ]ενονγαρπ..[
        ]ιναδηπ..κε[
        ]ευχομ...λ.[
5          ].ονε.[.]λκ.[
           ]ος   [
           ].ν..[
                      ·      ·
```

Fr. 16 1 ..[, the left-hand arc of a circle, followed by two dots on the line on a single fibre; ε.[or ο.[likely, but I cannot say that ω[is impossible　　2 ..[, the base of a circle with a tail at its right-hand end, followed by a short stroke at mid-letter descending from left; ου and perhaps εν appear to be acceptable　　3]ι close to the edge, ν not ruled out　　Of δ only the apex and lower end of right-hand stroke, λ not ruled out　　After π what looks like ρ but may be a cancelled ι; this is followed by a short arc from the lower left-hand side of a circle and an upright　　4 After μ what now looks like the foot of a concave stroke, but perhaps displaced　　Before λ the right-hand stroke of α or λ, after λ the start of a stroke rising to right　　5]., the top of a circle　　.[, the left-hand arc of a circle　　.[, an upright　　6]ο unusually narrow, but not, I think,].ι　　7]., perhaps the apex of α, though the upper part of the right-hand stroke is anomalously upright　　..[, the apex of a triangle, followed by the top of a circle

Fr. 17

```
        ].αδεγωπαραθηϲω
       ]..γα[]ϲκαλοιδωριαιϲ
            ]
            ].θων
5          ].οιϲιεροιϲιν
          ]εμνοπροϲωπον
           ].ικακοιϲιν
           ]..[]...[]ι
               ]..η
10            ]ηϲε.[ ]
            ]αρανηρ[
                ·    ·     ·
```

Fr. 17 1]., the lower end of a stroke curving down from left　　2].., apparently ϲ followed by the upper part of an upright bending over to right at the top, but I am doubtful whether this is the correct combination. λη might just possibly be an alternative　　4]., the end of a stroke from left touching θ (of which the cross-stroke is barely represented) about the middle　　5]., the right-hand end of a cross-stroke touching ο a little below the top　　7]., traces compatible with the extreme ends of the cross-stroke and the turn-up of ε   8]..[, remains suggesting the apex of a triangular letter, followed by the upper parts of two uprights   ]...[, the apex of a triangular letter, followed at an interval by another, and this by the upper part of an upright bending over to left and having a speck to right nearly level with its top, e.g. ν   9].., three successive uprights hooked to right at the foot   Of η only elements of the upper part   10 .[, the lower part of a stroke hooked to right

Fr. 17 6 c]εμνοπρόcωπον not recorded till Eustathius, but the verb at Aristoph. *Nub.* 363.

Fr. 18

]..[

]τι.η[

]ινηθε.[

].αcινc[

5   ]οcβιαν[

]εοντιν[

]..νδε.[

]ινπρ[

]cc[

10   ]cκε[

]ανδ[

·   ·   ·

Fr. 18 1]..[, on the line a horizontal stroke touching the foot of an upright   2 Between ι and η an apparently undamaged space blank except for a horizontal stroke attached to the top of the left-hand upright of η   3 .[, the lower left-hand arc of a circle   4]., two traces compatible with the right-hand side of the loop of φ   7]., on the line a dot, a short flat stroke, the base of a circle   .[, the thickened top of an upright, perhaps the left-hand stroke of ω   11 Of]α only the extreme end of the tail

Fr. 19

(a)   (b)

]διδ.[   ]...πρωτεμ[

].κο.[   ]ηνανδρ..[

]ερωτα[].[

]πλειcταταυ[

5   ]ηνδ[.].αμ[

].ωνο[.]κ[

]ει.[   ].[

·   ·   ·

Fr. 19 The cross-fibres fix the level of (b) relatively to (a) and I do not think there is any doubt that (b) stood to right of (a). There is no external evidence about their interval.

1 .[, the left-hand half of a circle   ]..., the top of a slightly forward-sloping or convex stroke, followed by the apex of a triangle and an upright with foot hooked to right;]ναι seems acceptable 2]., an upright with foot hooked to right   .[, at an interval a dot level with the top of the letters; if the fragments touched, this dot would be in the position of the tip of the left-hand upright of η, but I do not think the signs in l. 1 can be combined in a way to suit this location   ..[, a speck level with the top of the letters, followed at an interval by a short arc from the top left-hand side of a circle at about the same level   5]., a short piece near the line of a stroke descending from left   6]., the right-hand part of a cross-stroke touching the top of ω and a speck below it on the line   7 For]ϵ perhaps θ   ι headless; τ might be possible   .[, the lower left-hand arc of a circle

Fr. 20

]τιϲ...[
]ον.ọ[
]
]ρεινω[
5   ]   [
]ο[

.   .   .

Fr. 20 1 After ϲ the left-hand parts of ϵ or θ   ..[, the foot of an upright with a horizontal trace, off the line, to left, followed by the left-hand base angle of δ or ζ   2 After ν a speck level with the top of the letters, followed by an upright with foot hooked to right; if η, what I have taken for a damaged ο might be ϲ   6 The left-hand side of ο is anomalously thickened

Fr. 21

]δεδραϲ[
]νμεδειν.[
]κραγηνα[

.   .

Fr. 21 2 Of]ν only the lower right-hand parts;].ι may be possible   .[, the left-hand arc of a circle

Fr. 22

].παρατι.[
].υϲαϲεχ.[
]ν[   ]καθ[
]ϵ̣ι[   ]φ.[
5   ].[
].[

.   .   .

Fr. 22 1]., the right-hand end of a cross-stroke, touching an upright with foot hooked to right just below the top; perhaps η, but I think].ι likelier   .[, the lower part of a convex stroke with a dot above and to left   2]., the top of a circle; specks below are on the underlayer   .[, ϵ or θ   4 .[, the top of an upright   5 Now looks like the cusp of ω, but the surface is partly destroyed   6 The central part of the cusp of ω with a dot to left; nearly all on the underlayer

Fr. 23

]δειμο[

]ουδεγ[

]τοιαδ[

.   .   .

Fr. 24

.   .

]υχα[

]αζωδ..[

]ινϲεαυτ[

].ελληιϲμα[

5   ]ηϲιδιον.[

]ϵινεϲθ'οπ[

]ιϲτουϲαν[

]ππϵ....[

.   .   .

Fr. 24 2 ..[, the base of a circle, followed by the base of a circle; not ω   3 Of τ[only the left-hand end of the cross-stroke   4]., on the line the turn-up of a stroke; μ suits   5 .[, the left-hand parts of π or τ   6 Of]ϵ only the right-hand tip of the cross-stroke, but I think ϵι, not η 7 ο anomalous   8 Of]π only the top-right-hand angle   After ϵ the top of a circle, followed by the top of a circle   ..[, the upper end of a stroke descending to right, followed at an interval by a speck at the same level

Fr. 25

.   .   .

]   υφ[

]   θρ.[

]   ταχ[

]   χϵρα[

5   ]   οιλ.[

]ποι[

]ξυ[

.   .   .

Fr. 25 2 .[, the left-hand arc of a circle with its foot hooked to right below the line   5 .[, on the edge a slightly forward-sloping stroke

Fr. 26

.   .   .

].[

].κ..[ ]ν [

]ωcυδωρμαχηνξ[

]θοντιμηδοπωc.[

5   ]κανδιcωcκροτη[

].cεχοιτạνουφο[

]ριτριμμακακ[

]ọκυρβι.[

].'εικρατ[

10   ].κοτω[

].θωγ[

.   .   .

Fr. 26 2]., a dot level with the top of the letters, followed by the foot of a stroke hooked to right; perhaps two letters represented   ..[, the lower parts of λα suggested, but the papyrus is dark and encrusted   4 .[, an upright close to c; I suppose γ or π   6]., the lower end of a slightly concave upright   8 .[, a horizontal stroke on the line with a dot above its left-hand end; I cannot recognize part of any letter   9]., traces of ink, but too dark and encrusted to suggest a reading   I am not sure whether there is ink between ι and κ, which would make γκ a possible alternative   10]., the top left-hand arc of a circle   11]., the lower right-hand arc of a circle

Fr. 26 5 See 7 seq.

7 seq. περίτριμμα and κύρβιc applied to persons clever at taking advantage of the law Aristoph. *Nub.* 447 seq. A similar word for a cunning person was κρότημα. See Blaydes on *Nub.* l.c. and 260, Pearson on Soph. fr. 913.

Fr. 27

.   .   .

].[

].ου[

].cθεγ[

]c.[

.   .   .

Fr. 27 1 The lower left-hand part of ε or θ   2]., if the right-hand side of π, unusually small 3]., the right-hand arc of a circle   4 .[, the start of a stroke curving up to right

Frr. 28–31 are in one hand. If the writer is the same as the writer of the other fragments he has adopted a more elegant script. The recurrence of the original style in fr. 28, 7 seems to make it clear that there existed a relationship between the two groups.

Fr. 28

```
        ·    ·      ·
      ].ọϲ.[
      ].ι    [
         ]
         ]
5        ]
      ]ειται [
      ]παντο[
      Blank
```

Fr. 28 1]., the lower end of a stroke curving down from left   .[, a dot on the line   2].,
on the line the end of a stroke from left   7 το a small specimen of the same hand as wrote το
at, e.g., fr. 8, 7

Fr. 29

```
      ].ηδ[
      ].[].[
      ]μυϲο[
      ]...[
        ·      ·
```

Fr. 29 2].[, the apex of a triangle   ].[, a flat trace on the line   4].., a cross-stroke as of τ,
followed by the top of a circle

Fr. 30

```
        ·    ·      ·
      ]ερου    [
      ]μην    [
      ].ι      [
      ]ọϲ      [
5     ].θọ...[] [
        ·    ·     ·
```

Fr. 30 3]., the tip and the lower end of a stroke curving down from left   4 Of]ọ only the
right-hand half; ω perhaps possible   5]., the top of an upright   ...[, the upper ends of four
uprights, the first with a projection to left, the last with a detached trace to right; the combination,
and so the number of letters, uncertain

Fr. 31

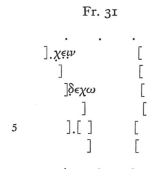

5

Fr. 31 1]., the turn-up of ε or ϲ   5 The base of a circle

2744. COMMENTARY

I can give no satisfactory account of the composition represented by the following remnants of two consecutive columns. There is recognizable a disquisition of considerable length (over fifty and perhaps over sixty lines) about the bird called τέτριξ and its habitat, apparently described as βολαῖα in the text commented on, though the commentary adduces only βολεῶνες, preceded by another of unknown length and of subject known only in so far as the word χλούνης appears to be relevant to it. A peculiarity of the piece is the three quotations from Aristotle, of which it would be supposed, on the analogy of the usual layout of commentaries, that two were lemmata, though it is quickly plain that they are no such thing, but, like the normally positioned passage of Deinarchus, corroborative matter.

What work, and whether prose or verse, was considered to require such elaborate exposition it is unprofitable on the basis of the two or three surviving words to conjecture.

The roll from which this fragment comes was about 10¼ inches in height with good margins above and below the column. The writing is an upright rounded book-hand of a not uncommon type, comparable with, e.g., **2245** and assignable to the second century.

Col. i

```
                                       ]αγριωϝοι
                                       ]χα
                           ]ροιωσπερομηροσεποι
                           ]ωρϲενεπιχλουϝηνϲυν
5                          ]νουδεεωικειαϝδριγεϲι
                           ]ωιαλλαριω[.]υληεντι γει
                    ]νονταιδεεκτομαιδιατονεοιϲ
                    ]υϲινεμπεπτειννοϲημακνιϲ
                    ]ονειϲτουϲορχειϲειταξυομε
10                                 ]κθλ[..]β[  ]υϲ
                                            ]δειϲ
                                            ]αυδα
                                              ]ϲ
                                                ]
15                                              ]
                                         ].οινον
                                           ]περ
                                    ]ε.ει.[].
                                        ].υϲτι
20                                      ]τετριξ
                                              ]
                                              ]
                                          ]νηι
                                        ].ων
25                                      ]οφω̄
                                        ]ακαι
                                        ]...
                                        ]...ω
                                        ].επει
30                                      ]ακαι [   ]
                                        ]ουτο
                                        ]αρκα.
                                         ]τε.
                                        ]..[ ]
35                                        ]ō
                                        ]ωι
                                        ]δε
                                        ]ουϲῑ
```

τῶν δ' ἀρρένων καὶ] ἀγρίων οἱ
τομίαι μείζους γείνονται καὶ] χα-
λεπώτε]ροι, ὥσπερ Ὅμηρος ἐποί-
ηϲεν·] ὦρϲεν ἔπι χλούνην ϲῦν
ἄγριο]ν οὐδὲ ἐώικει ἀνδρί γε ϲι-
τοφάγ]ωι ἀλλὰ ῥίω[ι] ὑλήεντι. γί-
νονται δὲ ἐκτομίαι διὰ τὸ νέοις
ο]ὖϲιν ἐμπίπτειν νόϲημα κνιϲ-
μ]ὸν εἰϲ τοὺϲ ὄρχειϲ, εἶτα ξυόμε-
νοι πρὸϲ τὰ δένδρα ἐ]κθλ[ί]β[ουϲι το]ὺϲ
ὄρχειϲ   ]δειϲ κτλ.

5

10

ἡ]δὲ
τέτριξ, ἣν Ἀθηναῖοι καλ]οῦϲιν

Col. ii

τραγαουτεεπιτηϲγηϲνοττ̣[
ειουτεπιτοιϲδενδρεϲιναλλε[
τοιϲχαμα̣[..]ζηλοιϲ καιμηποτα[
ριϲτοφα[..]ϲενορνειϲιν[
5 τηντετρα̣κα̣λεγει τε̣[.]ρα̣κ̣[
ταωνιβολαιαδεδ[.]νατα̣ι̣
τουϲ[.]ορβορωδ[...]τοπου.[
τ̣[   ]δ..οιϲμαλ̣ιϲτακα[
κοποιον...πειαινεταιβ̣ο̣[
10 .[.]α̣ϲδεκαιτουϲκοπρεω[
να̣ϲκαλειϲθαιφηϲιψαμερ[
α̣ϲδειναρχο̣ϲδεεντωικατα[
πολυε.[.].ουκεχρηταιτωιονο[
ματι̣[..]τωϲτοευρυϲακειον[
15 ενταυθαε̣[.].απε[...]ε̣πτακο̣[
ϲιαϲδρα̣χ[.]αϲυπερτηϲκοπρ[
ηνφαϲιν̣ο̣[.]εεδ̣ω̣[..]κα̣ια̣λε̣[
ξανδρουτ[.]νεξοιουκαιτωναλ[
λωντωντουϲβολε.[..].κε[
20 κτημενων.τιδεντοιϲτοι̣ο̣[
τοιϲτοποιϲδι̣[.]τρειβει̣δηλω[
ϲεικαιαριϲτοτελ̣ηϲκαιτην[
αιτιανπρ[.]ϲτ̣[.].ειϲεναπορ[
μα̣ϲινουτω[.]διατι̣[.]...ι̣ϲ[
25 δυϲωδεϲιχαιρε[.]η̣[.].ατοπλατυη[
εχειντονη̣[.].[.].ρακαιο.κ[.].υ̣[
ουκαιϲθητικ[..]ε̣ϲτι̣δια[.]...[
αι.[.]....κο̣.[...]...κε..[
π[.]ο̣ϲταϲοϲ.αϲ□ωϲπ.[
30 φλυγεϲτοιϲ[..]αυ..[.].οινο.[
[   ].□καιαυτηται̣ϲ....θ..μ.[...]..[
μαι.καιϲαπραιϲα̣ιτοιαυτα[.]...α̣[ ][
πτονταιει....α̣....εν.[   ]..[
τηϲμε.□.λ.[   ].δια[   ]..□.[
35 τοι[   ]ατ̣ο̣π[ ]ν..α..[.].[
τα.[   ].ρω[ ].η.ο.[
α[   ]ο̣ϲοβολ.[...].ϲιν.[
.α[   ]αετ.μυνκαιβο..[

τραγα, οὔτε ἐπὶ τῆς γῆς νοττ[εύ-
ει οὔτ' ἐπὶ τοῖς δένδρεσιν ἀλλ' ἐ[πὶ
τοῖς χαμαιζήλοις ⟨φυτοῖς⟩. καὶ μήποτ' Ἀ-
ριστοφά[νη]ς ἐν "Ορνισιν [αὐ-
5   τὴν τέτρακα λέγει· τέ[τ]ρακ[ι καὶ
ταῶνι. βολαῖα δὲ δ[ύ]ναται [
τοὺς [β]ορβορώδ[εις] τόπους [
τ[....]δ..οις μάλιστα κα[-
κοποιὸν... πιαίνεται. βο[λε-
10   ῶ[ν]ας δὲ καὶ τοὺς κοπρεῶ-
νας καλεῖσθαί φησιν Ἀμερ[ί-
ας. Δείναρχος δὲ ἐν τῶι κατὰ
Πολυεύ[κ]του κέχρηται τῶι ὀνό-
ματι [τού]τωι· τὸ Εὐρυσάκειον
15   ἐνταῦθα ε[ ].απε[...] ἑπτακο-
σίας δραχ[μ]ὰς ὑπὲρ τῆς κόπρ[ου
ἥν φασιν ο[.]εεδω[..] καὶ Ἀλε-
ξάνδρου τ[ο]ῦ ἐξ Οἴου καὶ τῶν ἀλ-
λων τῶν τοὺς βολεῶ[να]ς κε-
20   κτημένων. ὅτι δ' ἐν τοῖς τοιο[ύ-
τοις τόποις δι[α]τρίβει δηλώ-
σει καὶ Ἀριστοτέλης καὶ τὴν
αἰτίαν πρ[ο]στ[ι]θεὶς ἐν Ἀπορ[ή-
μασιν οὕτω[ς]· διὰ τί .[.]..οις
25   δυσώδεσι χαίρε[ι]; ἢ [δ]ιὰ τὸ πλατὺν
ἔχειν τὸν ν[.].[.]ηρα καὶ οὐκ[.].υ[
οὐκ αἰσθητικ[ός] ἐστι, διὰ [δ]ὲ τὸ[
αι.[.]..τικο.[...]...κε..[
π[ρ]ὸς τὰς ὀσμάς, ὥσπε[ρ οἱ οἰνό-
30   φλυγες τοῖς [..]αυ..[.].οινο.[
[   ].[ ]καὶ αὐτὴ ταῖς διεφθαρμέ[ναις ὀς-
μαῖς καὶ σαπραῖς. αἱ τοιαῦτα[ι].ρα[
πτονται ει....ατημεν.[   ]..[
της με.[ ].λυ[ ]..δια[   ]..[].[
35   τοι[   ]ατοπ[ ]ν..α..[.].[
τα.[   ].ρω[ ].η.οτ[
α[   ]οσοβολο[...].cιν.[
.α[   ]αετ.μυνκαιβο..[

Col. i 1 seqq. Aristot. *Hist. an.* 578ª32 seqq.   3 ὥϲπερ καί Ar.   4 θρέψεν Ar.   5 θηρί
Ar.   7 τομίαι 8 κνηϲ- Ar. codd. praeter Cª, P   16]., two dots in the positions of the
ends of the arms of κ   18 Between ϵ and ϵ perhaps ν   .[, an upright   19]., the lower right-
hand arc of a circle   24]., below the line the lower end of an upright, at mid-letter to right the
right-hand end of a stroke from left   27]..., the upper end of a stroke descending to right closely
followed by the upper left-hand arc of a small circle; then two traces compatible with the top of
a circle; e.g. ωϲϵ   28]..., the top of a circle, perhaps followed by a single ν ligatured to ω
32 After α the lower end of an upright below the line   33 After ϵ faint traces compatible with the
top of ϲ   34 An upright with ink to left a little above its foot, followed by the left-hand parts of
a circle   37 seq. Aristot. *Hist. an.* 559ª11 seq.   38 καλοῦϲιν Ἀθηναῖοι Ar. codd. praeter P,
Dª, Eª (οἱ Ἀθ.)

Col. ii 1 seqq. Aristot. *Hist. an.* 559ª12 seqq.   1 οὔραγα Ar.   3 φυτοῖϲ from Ar.
5 seq. Aristoph. *Av.* 885   8 After δ the left-hand arc of a circle, followed by the right-hand part
of a cross-stroke, level with the top of the letters, having a dot below on the line   9 ..., δια
appears acceptable, but the first two letters are represented only by faint traces on the line; of α perhaps the lower end of the loop and the lower end of the right-hand stroke   14 τωϲ ϲ has ι written
through it by the same hand   15]., a dot to left of the loop of α   17 Between α and ι
a trace off the line not accounted for   24 .[.].., dots on the line   26].[, the top of an
upright   ]., the right-hand stroke of δ or λ   28 .[.].., the first letter is represented by a dot
level with the top of the letters and a dot on the line below and to right, the rest by traces on the line
.[, a dot on the line   ]..., perhaps the right-hand parts of δ, followed by the top of ι and this by the
lower end of the right-hand stroke of α   .[, the foot of an upright, followed by a trace below the
line   30 ..[, the upper end of a stroke descending to right with a dot below and to right, followed
by a short arc of the base of a circle on the line with a dot above and to right   ]., a short horizontal
stroke with a detached dot at its left-hand end, level with the top of the letters, and a dot below on the
line   .[, a dot on the line   31].[, a dot level with the top of the letters   ]..[, two traces with
a space between them which I can bring into no particular relation with the supplements   32].,
a dot at mid-letter   33 Between ι and α the lower right-hand arc of a circle, the upper right-hand
arc of a circle, the top of an upright, the right-hand end of a cross-stroke level with the top of the
letters   .[, the left-hand end of a cross-stroke as of τ   ]..[, perhaps the loop of ρ, followed by γ or
the left-hand parts of π   34 .[, a dot on the line   ]., a dot at mid-letter   ].., disjointed
traces, close enough together to be parts of one letter, but I cannot combine them   ]..[].[, the tops
of two uprights with a dot between, not prima facie ν, followed at an interval by the top of a circle
35]ατοπ[and in l. 36].ρω[are on a detached scrap of which the vertical fibres can be followed with
certainty but I cannot follow the horizontal fibres either to right or to left   After ν two dots in the
positions of the top and bottom of an upright, followed by a trace a little off the line   After α perhaps the top and base of ϲ, followed by the foot of an upright   ].[, a flat stroke on the line   36 .[,
the upper end of a stroke descending to right   ]., the upper part of an upright   Before η the right-
hand stroke of δ or λ, after η perhaps π or τι   36 seq. Between these lines the top of a small
circle, not suggesting any part of a paragraphus, though approximately in the appropriate position
37]., apparently a cancelled letter   .[, the lower left-hand curve of the left-hand loop of φ suggested, but at a lower level than elsewhere   38 The first letter looks like κ lacking its lower arm;
perhaps a badly made γ   Between τ and μ the lower right-hand arc of a circle, prima facie ο   ..[,
two dots compatible with the feet of λ, followed by the left-hand arc of a circle

Col. i 1 seqq. I suppose part of a comment on χλούνηϲ which is etymologized and interpreted in
various ways. Cf. Eustath. as below, schol. B *Il.* ibid.
3 seq. Ὅμηροϲ ἐποίηϲεν At *Il.* ix 539 is found ὦρϲεν ἔπι χλούνην ϲῦν ἄγριον ἀργιόδοντα. This is
quoted by Aristotle and, according to Eustathius ad loc., by Strabo in the form θρέψεν . . . ἄγριον,
οὐδὲ ἐῴκει followed by a line not in our *Iliad*, θηρί γε ϲιτοφάγωι, κτλ. This commentary in quoting
Aristotle credits him with the more appropriate ὦρϲεν but imports the absurd ἀνδρί from *Od.* ix 191.
8 ἐμπεπτειν No doubt the copyist has written an upright too few and meant -πείπτειν.
20 The comment on the τέτριξ and its habits, presumably including a mention of βολαῖα, starts or
has started as far away from Col. ii as this.

37 seq.—ii 3 I know of no way of deciding between οὔραγα and τραγα. Nemesianus (i 128) says that in Rome they took to calling the *tetrax tarax*.

In view of οὔτε ἐπὶ τῆς γῆς so shortly before I suppose ἐπὶ τοῖς χαμαιζήλοις cannot be accepted without the addition of φυτοῖς. But there is an inconsistency in Aristotle himself; a little earlier he had said that, like quails and partridges, the lark and the τέτριξ lay their eggs on the ground.

3 seqq. 'Perhaps Aristophanes means this bird by τέτραξ in τέτρακι καὶ ταῶνι *Birds*' l. 885.

6 seqq. βολαῖα unattested.

I can make no guess at the relevance of ll. 8 seq. nor even at the construction. δ' ἐν τοῖς would remove one difficulty, but though δε τοις is a likely reading, δ εν τοις is not a possible one.

9 seqq. βολεῶνας Harpocr. 74, 4 ὁ τόπος ὅπου ἡ κόπρος βάλλεται βολεών καλεῖται. Νίκανδρος ἐν γ Ἀττικῆς διαλέκτου· βολεῶνας ἐπὶ τῶν ἄγρων, εἰς οὓς τὰ κόπρια ἐκφέρει. οὕτω Δείναρχος (see l. 12) καὶ Φιλήμων καὶ ἄλλοι. Similarly Eustath. 1404 fin. ὁ βολεών Ἀττικῶς ὅ ἐστι κοπρών ἤτοι κοπροβολεῖον, Pollux vii 134, *Et. Mag.* 204, 25.

κοπρέων for κοπρών apparently first in Tzetz. *Chil.* vi 520.

Ἀμερίας sc. ὁ Μακεδὼν ἐν ταῖς Γλώσσαις, known largely from Athenaeus and Hesychius.

12 seq. Deinarchus seems to have made at least four speeches against Polyeuctus.

14 Apparently οὕτως corrected by the same hand to τούτωι, though [του] looks rather crushed and there is now no sign of a superscript τ.

14 seqq. I cannot follow the construction of the quotation as a whole. I can guess nothing more plausible than that somebody is said to have bought 700 drachmas worth of manure from the owners of the Athens sewage.

τὸ Εὐρυσάκειον ἐνταῦθα: the shrine of Eurysakes was in the Agora. Here (Pollux) or hereabouts (Harpocr.) congregated men looking for a job, among them κοπροφόροι. See Harpocr. in Κολωνέτας, Pollux vii 132 seqq.

ἐξ Οἴου Οἶον was the name of two Attic demes, Harpocr. in v. The δημοτικόν is regularly ἐξ Οἴου, e.g. Dem. π. Μακάρτ. 3, Aeschin. κ. Κτης. 115 (Steph. Byz. in Μετάχοιον and Ἀβρότονον).

κεκτημένων To judge by Dem. κ. Ἀριστογείτ. the κοπρώνων ἐπιστάται (i.e., I suppose, the ἀστυνόμοι) were elective. From κεκτημένων I should infer that Alexander and his associates had purchased the contract for the disposal of the sewage.

21 διατρίβει sc. ἡ τέτριξ.

23 seq. ἐν Ἀπορήμασιν To judge by the quotation the treatise here called ἀπορήματα must have resembled, if it was not the same as, the work often referred to as φυσικὰ προβλήματα. The extant Προβλήματα have nothing about the τέτριξ (though a good deal about drunkards).

24 I can make no suggestion for the accommodation of the remaining traces to the required sense. The τέτριξ was not named.

25 seqq. 'Because it has a broad — and not a — one, it is not sensitive.'

I can find no appropriate noun beginning with ν. Of μ[υ]κ[τ]ηρα, which would not seem out of place, I am bound to say that μ was not written.

The antithesis to 'broad' should be verifiable, but I have not lighted on it.

Of the τέτριξ -κ[ή] would be expected. The available space appears to require more than η. -κός presumably applies to ν-ηρ.

27 seqq. διὰ δὲ τὸ . . . διακεῖσθαι πρὸς τὰς ὀσμάς looks probable (though I am bound to say that the natural interpretation of the faint trace after κει is not ς), but this requires an adverb and I cannot make -κως out of the ink at the end of the first word of l. 28. [μὴ | αἰσθητικῶς might be an approximation to the sense, but -σθη- is not what was written between αι and τι.

29 seqq. I can suggest nothing better in l. 30 than φαύλοις, though I cannot verify λο and ς is very unsatisfactory. 'As drunkards like wines that have gone off, she likes corrupt and rotten smells.' The verb supplied from l. 25.

I have no parallel to διεφθαρμέναις ὀσμαῖς for 'smells of corruption' and perhaps διεφθαρμένων is preferable. σαπραὶ ὀσμαί Aristot. π. αἰσθ. 433ᵇ11.

37 seq. The two quotations from Aristotle, 1 seqq. and 24 seqq., but not that from Deinarchus, 14 seqq., project into the left-hand margin. The beginning of the second of the two—the beginning of the first is not preserved—is also indicated by a paragraphus. But I do not know what significance

these facts have in relation to 37 seq., which do not project, but are aligned with the commentary 4–24, and have some mark, but not prima facie a paragraphus, which separates them from what precedes.

As a general rule, if any lines in a commentary project, it is the lemma which projects and the exposition which is indented. Although there are in this piece three passages from Aristotle of which two certainly project, it is impossible to interpret them as lemmata, the last particularly being obviously a quotation adduced to support the exposition.

ADDENDUM TO **2740**. COMMENTARY ON EUPOLIS *Ταξίαρχοι* ?

The following set of fragments is in the same hand as **2740**, which there is reason to describe as a commentary on the *Ταξίαρχοι* of Eupolis, and may well have formed part of the same commentary. On the other hand, the two groups were found separately and, though it is probable that both (if either) relate to Eupolis, they need not both relate to the same comedy. I have found no physical connexion between them. As none of the commentary and only a couple of words of the lemmata are recoverable the question is of no present importance.

Fr. 1

	Col. i	Col. ii
	]δι	κακη[
	]φει	γραψ[
	].υ	δετη[
	].αςταν	δες.[
5	].ρι	των[
	].τηι	δεδρα[
	].φηςιν	τωιτη[
	]α	ωςοδε[
	].ν	ξενοκ[
10	].γ	τοιδε[
	]εο	ποιη[
	]αι	οδερ[
	].ν	τωνδε [
	]ν	̲.̲.̲.ιειρη[
15	].ν	πεπληκτ[
	]	ταπαριςτ[
	]	χροτητ[
	]	τωιμ[
	].ν	κο.[.]ςαι[
20	]ηι [	] ν[ ] [

Fr. 1 Col. i 3]., perhaps the foot of the right-hand upright of ν   4]., there appears to be the end of a cross-stroke touching the top of α but I am not sure that a letter is represented   5]., what resembles a semicircle slightly tilted to left; perhaps κ   6]., two dots on the line. If a single η or ν, γ might be preferable to τ   9]., ο suggested but ω not ruled out   15]., at mid-letter a slightly concave stroke

Col. ii 4 .[, off the line a loop open to right; if φ, anomalous   14 . . ., the foot of an upright, followed by the tops of two uprights and these at a slightly greater than usual interval by a dot on the line   19 .[, an upright, followed by a dot level with its top

Fr. 1 Col. ii 9 ξενοκ[there is a reasonable chance that Xenocles, the son of Carcinus, is to be recognized. He is mentioned disparagingly by Aristophanes more than once and by Plato the comedian in his Σοφιϲταί.

15 seq. Lemma.

19 I think κον[.]ϲαι likelier than κομ[.]ϲαι[.

Fr. 2

```
         ·              ·
            ]ειν[
            ]ογ.[
            ]αυτ[
          ].αιτ.[
    5     ]ποτω[
           ].ει.[
             ]δ[
            ]ε.[
           ].υ[
         ·        ·        ·
```

Fr. 2 2 ọ would be read θ   .[, the lower part of an upright   3 υ anomalous; if τ intended, badly made   4]., the right-hand part of a cross-stroke touching the top of the loop of α   .[, the base of a circle   6]., a dot level with the top of the letters   .[, the tip of an upright serifed to left   8 .[, the lower part of an upright   9]., the right-hand ends of the branches of κ or χ

Fr. 3

```
       ·        ·
          ]ν[]τ̣[
          ]ντ.[
          ]ηϲει̣[
          ]ε̣.κω[
          ]τουϲ[
          ]νοιμω[
          ]πον[
       ·        ·        ·
```

Fr. 3 2 .[, a short arc from the upper left-hand side of a circle   4 Before κ a dot on the line and a speck above it level with the top of the letters

Fr. 4   Fr. 5

                                    Col. i   Col. ii

                               1][]ω   [
(a)

]νυμοιλεπ.[   ].ι   [[αρ]ιϲ[

(b)].ϲφι..[   ]   δα[

].[ ]ντοδ[   ] εγε[

]ι.ε.[   ] πο[

5   ]ηδημο[ ].αγνωϲε[5   ] τω.[

]αχθοιτει[ ].αϲτρεφ[   ] τιαικαια.[

].[ ].οφ.[ ].ιοναγ[   ].εγ..[

].[

].ο.[

10]νη[

]α̣[

Frr. 4 (*a*), **5** The fibres run across from fr. 4 (*a*) to fr. 5 and it is probable that two consecutive columns are represented. I cannot verify what I believe to be the relation of fr. 4 (*b*) to fr. 4 (*a*), that it stands to left of (*a*) 5 seqq. and that no whole letter is lost between them in the first and third of their common lines

Fr. 4 1 .[, the middle of an upright; the spacing suggests τ   2]., a faint dot on the line ..[, the apex and a trace to left on the line of a triangular letter, followed by the top left-hand arc of a circle   4 Of]ι only the top and foot. It is followed by the apex of a triangular letter   .[, the upper ends of two not quite parallel strokes descending to right, having to right the end of a cross-stroke and below a dot on the line   5]., an upright   6]., an upright   7 (*b*)].[, the tip of an upright (a comma-like mark just below seems to be on the underlayer)   ]., the lower end of a stroke curving down from left, e.g. λ, μ   .[, the lower left-hand arc of a circle   (*a*)]. the upper right-hand arc of a circle, against it the top of a loop with what looks like a small 'circumflex' on the line below   8 The apex of a triangular letter (the preceding traces on the underlayer)   9]., the upper part of a slightly backward-sloping upright   .[, the upper part of an upright   11 Perhaps]να̣[should be written, to account for the backward curve of the top of the left-hand stroke of α̣

Fr. 4 If I am right about the relation of (*b*) to (*a*), a satisfactory text emerges in l. 6, ἂν] ἄχθοιτ' εἰ [δ]ιαϲτρέφ[οιτο, an acceptable text in l. 5, however articulated. The difficulty presented by l. 7 is not primarily due to the juxtaposition but to signs on (*a*) alone.

5 μον seems likely, though not verifiable. There is nothing to guide one's choice among the possible ways of dividing the letters. Δῆμος (ὁ Πυριλάμπους, mentioned, as well as by Aristophanes, *Vesp.* 98, where see Blaydes's note, by Eupolis ἐν Πόλεϲιν, fr. 213) is to be remembered.

6 'Would be annoyed, if he were . . .'. For διαϲτρέφοιτο cf. fr. 11. 1; 8; 11 of the play identified as the Δῆμοι of Eupolis, where the meaning is not certain. In Aristophanes, who has the word several times, it appears to be 'get a squint'.

7 On the hypothesis .οφω.ιον would have to be the rendering of the signs. The ink after ω resembles no recognizable letter, ρ perhaps the nearest, and looks as if it had been inserted by the original hand.

Fr. 5 Col. i 1]., the lower end of a stroke curving down from left to touch ι above the foot

Col. ii 1 The top of ϲ is so elongated towards right that perhaps ϲτ[or the like should be written 5 .[, an upright   6 .[, partly faded traces, perhaps compatible with the top left-hand parts of ξ 7]., a cross-stroke touching ε a little below the top   ..[, dispersed traces of which the last suggests the top of the left-hand upright of ν

Fr. 6

Col. i   Col. ii

```
    .     .     .        .      .      .

      ].[  ]αν[
      ]δεͅδοι
      ].εφαι              [
                               [
      ]πλησι             [
                           δᾳ[
  5   ]ηλικην         [  ]κεκ[
      ]πλαςι            κ[
      ]..ςδε            ᾳ[
      ]...τοͅυ      5    φ.[
      ].ιᾳ[[ι]]ξεν       κω[
 10   ].ημου          [
      ].νςκω        [ ]....[
      ]λλευς       θωνιο.[
      ]καινε    10   μεχ[
      ]νιδος          .[
```

Fr. 6 Col. i 2 Of δ only the opposite ends of the base   3]., the upper end of the upper arm of κ suggested   7]. ., the base of ε or ϲ, followed by the foot of an upright hooked to right 8]. . ., apparently a flat stroke on the line, followed by a loop open upward and this by the start of a stroke rising to right   9]., perhaps a triangular letter, but the fibres are disturbed   10]., a stroke curving out from left and ending in an upright; there may be a trace a little below the middle on its left-hand side

Col. ii 2 Of κ only the outer end of the upper arm   5 .[, the left-hand arc of a circle 6 Above ω ink, not apparently a letter   8]. . ., the lower part of ε or ϲ, followed by the foot of a stroke hooked to right, and this by a light dot and the foot of an upright at a slightly higher level .[, on the line a loop open to right?   9 .[, traces compatible with the top and bottom of the left-hand side of ν   10 Of. χ[only elements of the left-hand side, but not, I think, λ   11 .[, the upper left-hand arc of a circle

Fr. 7

Col. i   Col. ii

.   .   .   .   .   .

                        ] π.δ[

                        ] η[].[.[

          ].   .[]...[

          ].ι $\delta\iota$.[

             5      $\tau\rho\alpha\gamma$.[

                        ] $\gamma\alpha$...[

.   .   .   .   .   .

Fr. 7 Rubbed and partly stripped. Perhaps from above fr. 6.

Col. ii 1 For π perhaps γ[.]   Before δ the lower part of an upright   2].., the lower right-hand arc of a circle, followed by the upper part of a stroke descending to right, with a dot below it on the line   3 .[, a dot level with the top of the letters   ]...[, the right-hand part of a cross-stroke with an upright descending from its right-hand end, followed by the top of a circle, and this by the upper tip of a stroke descending to right   4 .[, a trace (of the left-hand arc of a circle?) a little above mid-letter   5 .[, the left-hand arc of a circle   6 Of $\gamma\alpha$ only the cross-stroke and the apex   ...[, the ink could be taken as representing χ, υ, τ (or π)

Fr. 8

.   .   .

      ]. $\kappa\alpha\theta$[

      ]..$\nu\gamma$[

Blank with scattered specks
for about five lines

Fr. 8 A 'joint' near the left-hand edge.

2]., an upright well below the line with transverse traces at top; ϕ not suggested   Before ν faint traces near the top left-hand angle

Fr. 9

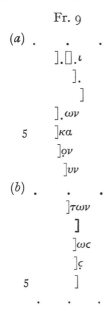

(a) .　.　.
].[].ι
].
]
].ων
5　]κα
]ον
]υν

(b) .　.　.
]των
]
]ως
]ϲ
5　]

.　.　.

Fr. 9 (a), (b) appear to come from the same column, I think in the order shown, I cannot tell at what distance apart.

(a) 1 The right-hand end of a cross-stroke is ligatured to the top of ι　　4]., the lower part of an upright

INDEX TO NEW CLASSICAL TEXTS

(The figures **27** are to be supplied before **33–44**; figures in small raised type refer to fragments, small roman figures to columns; an asterisk indicates that the word to which it is attached is not recorded in the ninth edition of Liddell and Scott, *Greek–English Lexicon*; square brackets indicate that a word is supplied from other sources or by conjecture; a reference enclosed in round brackets indicates an interlinear comment. The article is not indexed.)

(a) LYRIC, ETC. (2733–6)

ἀγαθός 33 7.
(-)ἄγειν 34 ¹¹ 7?
ἀγένητος [36 ¹ 12].
ἀγέρωχος 35 ²⁷ 14.
ἀγκυλότοξος 36 ¹ 16.
ἀγνοεῖν 34 ⁶ 4.
ἀγών 35 ¹ 37.
*ἀδειμαντομάχας [36 ²⁽ᵃ⁾ 7?].
ἀδιάλειπτος [34 ¹¹ 3?].
ἀδινός 35 ² 8.
ἀείδειν 35 [¹ 5], ⁶ 3.
ἀθάνατος [35 ³⁴ 12].
Ἀΐδης 36 ¹ 10.
αἶσα 35 ¹ 8   36 ²⁽ᵇ⁾ 7.
ἀκάτιον [34 ⁶ 3?].
ἀλκή [35 ²⁷ 3?].
ἄλλος 35 ¹ 27.
ἅλς 36 ²⁽ᵇ⁾ 11.
ἄλσος 35 ¹ 34.
ἀμοιβή [36 ¹ 19].
ἀμύνειν 36 ²⁽ᵃ⁾ 3.
ἀμφί 35 ¹ 33.
Ἀμφιτρυωνιάδης [36 ²⁽ᵇ⁾ 4].
ἀνά 35 ¹ 28?
ἀνάγκη 36 ²⁽ᵇ⁾ 4.
ἀναφέρειν [36 ²⁽ᵇ⁾ 12?].
ἄνεμος [34 ⁶ 7].
ἀνήρ 35 ⁸ 3?.
ἄνθρωπος [34 ¹ 7?] 36 ²⁽ᵇ⁾ 15.
ἀνίκητος 35 ¹¹ 14.
ἀντίθεος 35 ¹ 18.
]αντίμαχος 36 ²⁽ᵃ⁾ 2.
ἀοιδή 36 ¹ 17.
ἀοίδιμος [36 ³ 3].
ἀπειλεῖν 34 ¹ 16.
ἄπλατος [35 ¹¹ 3?].
Ἀπόλλων 34 ¹ [4?], [5], 15.
ἀργυρόπεζος 35 ² 9.
ἀρήιος 35 ¹¹ 9?
ἀρηΐφατος 36 ²⁽ᵃ⁾ 11.

ἀρήων 35 ²⁷ 3.
Ἀρι( ) (35 ³³ (3).
Ἀριστοτέλης [34 ⁴ 3?].
ἅρμα 35 ¹¹ 7.
ἄρχειν 36 ¹ 17.
ἀρχή [34 ¹ 11, 21].
ἀσφ[35 i 9?
Ἀσωπός [35 ¹ 37?].
ἄτε 35 ¹¹ 5.
αὖ 35 ¹ 23, ²⁷ 13 ?
αὐλητήρ [35 ¹ 5].
αὐτός 34 ¹ 16, ⁶ [2?], 6.
ἀφικνεῖσθαι [35 ⁴² 6].
ἄφρων 36 ¹ 11.
ἀχάεις see ἠχήεις.

βαθύς 35 ¹ 32.
(-)βαίνειν 35 ¹⁶ 8?
βέλος 35 ² 8.
βλέφαρον see γλέφαρον.
βου[34 ⁵ 5.
βουλή [36 ²⁽ᵇ⁾ 10?].

γαμεῖν 35 ¹¹ 6?
γάρ [34 ⁶ 7] 35 ³⁴ 8 36 ²⁽ᵇ⁾ 9.
Γαρυόνας see Γηρυόνης.
γενέθλιος 34 ¹ 14.
Γηρυόνης 35 ¹¹ 18.
γίγας 35 ²⁷ 2.
γίγνεσθαι 35 ² 10, ²⁷ 4 ?
γλέφαρον 36 ²⁽ᵇ⁾ 17.
γυνή 36 ²⁽ᵇ⁾ 6, 13.

δαΐζειν 36 ²⁽ᵃ⁾ 8.
δαίμων [35 ¹ 11?].
δακέθυμος [35 ⁴ 1].
δέ 34 ¹ 20, 21, ⁶ 8 35 ¹ 23, [40?], ¹¹ 4, 10?, 11, ²⁷ 13 ? 36 ²⁽ᵇ⁾ 4.
δειλός 33 3?
διά 36 ²⁽ᵃ⁾ 11.

διανοεῖν 34 ⁶ 6.
διδόναι 35 ¹ 12.
δοκεῖν 36 ¹ 15.
δολοπ[[35 ³⁴ 2].
δρόμος [35 ¹ 36?, ¹¹ 2?].
δύναμις 35 ¹ 10.
δυν[35 ¹¹ 13.
δύνασις (35 ¹ 10).

ἐγώ 34 ⁶ 5.
εἶδος [35 ¹ 26].
εἶναι 33 9 34 ⁴ 5?, ⁶ 5 35 ¹ 22.
εἰς 35 ¹ 37 36 ¹ 10?, 21.
ἐκ 36 ²⁽ᵇ⁾ 11.
ἐκτρέπειν 33 6.
ἐλεφαν- 35 ¹⁷ 8?
ἕλιγμα 35 ⁸ 5.
ἐν 35 ¹ 16.
ἐναλίγκιος 35 ¹ 26.
ἔνθεν 34 ⁶ 8.
ἔνιοι 33 13.
εντ[34 ⁶ 5.
ἑξῆς 33 9, 12.
ἐπί 35 ¹ 37, ⁶ 2.
ἐπιβαίνειν [35 ¹¹ 10?].
ἐπικρατής [35 ³⁴ 6].
ἐπικωμα[[35 ¹³ 5].
ἐπιχειρεῖν [34 ⁶ 9].
ἐπιχθόνιος [35 ¹ 25?].
ἐρασιπλόκαμος 36 ²⁽ᵇ⁾ 10.
ἐραστ[35 ¹⁶ 10.
ἐρευθ[35 ⁹ 5.
ἐρισφάραγος [36 ²⁽ᵃ⁾ 3?].
ἔρως 35 ¹ 7.
ἐς see εἰς.
ἐσσα[35 ¹ 41.
εὖ [33 10?].
ευ[35 ¹ 32?
εὐπατέρεια [35 ⁹ 2].
εὐπλόκαμος 36 ²⁽ᵃ⁾ 9.

τέλος **35** i 9?
τερψίμβροτος **36** 2(a) 5.
τεύχειν [**34** 1 22].
τιθέναι **36** 2(a) 6.
τις **35** 11 4　**36** 1 15?
τλᾶν **33** 8, 10.
τόξον **36** 2(a) 2.
]τραπετα[**35** 40 3.
Τραχίνιος [**36** 1 22].
τρέχειν [**35** 11 8].
τρίτος **34** 1 20.
Τυνδαρίδης **35** 1 15.
τυρανν[**34** 12(a) 6.
τυρα[νν- **34** 12(a) 9?
τυραννία **36** 2(b) 14?

υἱός **33** 11　**36** 2(a) 4.
ὑμνεῖν **34** 1 12.
ὑπέρτερος **35** 11 12.
ὑπό **35** 11 7.
ὑποΐζεσθαι [**36** 2(b) 11?].
ὕστατος [**36** 1 8].

φάναι **34** 1 22.
φατός **35** 1 22.
(-)φέρειν **33** 13.
φεύγειν **33** 14.
φοίνιος **35** 2 6.
φρήν **35** 6 2, (28 4).

χαιρ.[**36** 2(a) 12.

χαίρειν **34** 1 11.
χαλεπός **35** 11 4.
χάλκασπις **36** 1 22.
(-)χθών **35** 17 7.
χορός **35** 1 31.
χρόνος **34** 4 5.
χρύσαιγις **35** 1 20.
Χρυσάωρ **35** 11 17.
χρύσεος [**35** 17 5?].
χρυσοπέδιλος **36** 1 20.

ὦ **36** 2(b) 14?
ᾠδή [**34** 1 10?].
ὡς **35** [1 8?], 40 4.

(b) OLD COMEDY, ETC. (2737–43)

ἀγαθός **41** 1A ii 11　**43** 3 26.
ἄγαν **43** 8 ii 4.
ἀγορά **41** 5(a) ii 5.
ἀγορεύειν [**43** 8 ii 4?].
ἀγροικός **38** 4.
ἀγχ[**37** 2 24.
ἀεί see αἰεί.
Ἀθηνᾶ **38** 3, 5.
Αἶγες **38** 1.
αἰεί **42** 1 31.
Αἴσχυλος [**37** 2 21].
ἄκρος **42** 1 22?
ἀλετρίς [**41** 5(a) ii 9].
Ἀλκμάν **37** 1 i 25, ii 18.
Ἀλκμέων **41** 1B ii 10.
ἀλλά **37** 1 i 27 **41** 1A i 18, ii 22, 39　**42** 1 30.
αλλα **41** 1B iii 28, 29.
ἄλλος [**37** 1 ii 12]　**40** 1 9.
ἀλλότριος **41** 1B iii 24.
ἀμφότερος **40** 1 13　**41** 4 11.
ἄν **37** 1 i 12, 14　**41** 1C ii 10?　**43** 3 25, 8 ii 6, 11 3, 26 6.
ἀνάνθρωπος [**41** 1A ii 34?].
ἀνδρ.. **43** 19 2.
ἀνήρ **41** 4 13　[**43** 8 i 16].
ἀνθρω[π- **41** 1A ii 18.
ἄνθρωπος **41** 1A ii 34?
ἀνιέναι **43** 8 i 15?
ἀντέχειν [**43** 3 25].
ἀντί **40** 1 [12], 17, [20?], 2 i 20, ii [2], 11　**41** 1A i [14?], 30, 38　**43** 3 24.
ἄντικρυς **42** 1 24.

ἀντίπρωρον **41** 1B ii 4.
ἀξιοῦν **41** 1C ii 9.
ἀπαντλεῖν [**37** 1 i 8].
ἀπαρνεῖσθαι **41** 1B ii 2.
ἅπας **41** 1A i 32.
ἁπλοῦς **40** 2 i 21　**43** 8 i 7.
ἀπό **37** 1 i 3　**41** 1A i [16], 29, 1B iii 7　**42** 1 8　**43** 8 ii 1?
ἀποκλίνειν [**38** 13].
ἀπολλύναι **41** 1B iii 8.
ἀπορρυποῦν **43** 8 ii 1?
ἀπωθεῖν **37** 1 ii 16.
ἄρα **41** 1B ii 18　**43** 8 i 3, ii 1.
ἀργύρωμα [**41** 4 7].
Ἄρης **40** 1 14, 15.
Ἀριστάρχειος **37** 1 21.
Ἀριστοφάνης **37** 1 i 4　**38** 8　**42** 1 16.
ἀρκεῖν **38** 9, 11.
(-)αρκεῖν **41** 7 i 7.
ἀρκετός **40** 1 12?
ἀρχή **37** 1 i 23, ii 19, [2 21].
Ἀρχιλ[οχ- **41** 8 3.
ἀσαφής [**37** 1 i 13?].
ἀσθενεῖν **41** 1A i 11?
Ἀσπασία **41** 4 10.
Ἀτάλαντος [**42** 1 8].
ἀτεχνῶς **40** 2 i 22.
αὖθις **37** 1 i 8.
αὐλητής **42** 1 12.
αὐτοκάβδαλον [**41** 5(a) ii 7, 5(b) 2].
αὐτός **38** 7, 12　**41** 1A ii 7, 23, 1B ii 8, 9, iii 8, 4 12.
αὐτοῦ **37** 1 ii 14 see ἑαυτόν.

ἀφιέναι **41** 1A i 17.
ἄχθεσθαι **40** Add. 4 6.

βαδίζειν **40** 2 ii 5.
βαλανεύειν [**37** 1 i 6?].
βάλλειν **42** 1 20.
βαρύς **43** 8 ii 8.
βασιλεύς [**41** 5(a) i 7?].
βία **43** 18 5.
βλέπειν **43** 8 i 10.
(-)βλέπειν **43** 1 16.
Βουκόλοι **39** 6.
βούλεσθαι **37** 1 ii 22.
βράσσειν [**37** 1 ii 33].
βροτός **43** 8 i 7.

γάρ **40** 2 ii 4, 6　**41** 1A ii 7, 8, 18, 1B ii [6], 14, 20, iii 8, 1C ii 4, 8, 4 11　**42** 1 9　**43** 1 13, 3 16, 20, 26, 8 i 2?, 7, ii 4, 11 1?, 6, 16 2.
γε **40** 2 i 15　**41** 4 13.
Γηρυτάδης **42** 1 16.
γίγνεσθαι **37** 1 ii 15　**41** 1B ii 3　[**42** 1 9].
γιγνώσκειν **42** 1 27.
γλῶττα **41** 1B ii 5.
γνω[**40** 2 i 10.
γνώμη **41** 1C i 13.
γνώριμος **41** 1C ii 11.
*Γοργοδρακοντοδόκα **38** 10?
γοῦν **41** 1A i 18.
γραμματοδιδάσκαλος **41** 1A i 15, 16.

γράφειν [41 $^{5(a)}$ ii 7?] 40 Add.
^{1} ii 2.
γυνή 41 ^{1B} ii 20.

(-)δαίμων 43 ^{10} 5.
Δαιταλεῖς [37 ^{1} i 5].
δέ 37 ^{1} i 23, 24, 26, ii 2, 14, ^{2} 9?, 20?
   21 38 ^{1} 40 ^{1} 9 41 ^{1A} i 14, 16,
   18, 33, ii 20?, ^{1B} ii 1, 18, iii 2,
   12?, 17?, $^{5(a)}$ ii 10 42 ^{1} 4 43
   ^{3} 23, ^{8} i 10?, 11, ii 2, 5, 8, ^{17}
   2?, ^{26} 5.
δεδιέναι 41 ^{1B} iii 14.
δεῖν [41 ^{4} 10?].
δεῖν (to bind) 41 ^{1C} ii 10.
δέλτος 41 ^{1A} i 19.
δέος 43 ^{3} 16.
δέρμα 41 ^{1A} ii 16.
δεσπότης 41 [^{1B} iii 2], ^{1C} ii 7.
δεύτερος 41 ^{1A} ii 32.
δή 41 ^{1A} i 21 42 ^{1} 19 43 ^{3} 23.
Δηλιάδες 39 2.
δηλοῦν 38 12.
δῆμος 41 ^{1A} ii 41.
δῆτα 40 ^{2} i 19.
διά 37 ^{1} ii 4, 13 42 ^{1} 13.
*διακυσοςαλεύειν 43 ^{8} ii 3.
διαλύειν [37 ^{1} ii 34].
διαςθενεῖν 41 ^{1A} i 11?
διαστρέφειν [40 Add. ^{4} 6].
διατιθέναι 41 ^{1A} i 8.
διδάσκαλος 37 ^{1} ii 21 38 6.
διδάσκειν 37 ^{1} i 5, ii 14.
διδόναι 37 ^{1} i [28], ii 12 [41 ^{4}
   15?, $^{5(a)}$ ii 1].
(-)διδόναι 41 ^{1A} ii 26.
δικ[41 $^{5(a)}$ ii 4.
δίκαιος 37 ^{1} ii 19 43 ^{11} 6.
δίκη 43 ^{8} i 2.
Διοκλῆς 41 ^{4} 13, 14.
Διονύσια 37 ^{1} ii 9.
Διόνυσος 42 ^{1} 12 [43 ^{11} 4].
Διότιμος 37 ^{1} i 3.
Δίρκη 37 ^{2} 24.
δοκεῖν [37 ^{1} i 21?] 40 ^{1} 11.
]δουλο[41 ^{1B} ii 24.
δοῦλος 41 ^{1B} ii 21.
δρᾶμα 37 ^{2} 12?
Δραπέτιδες 39 5.
δυν[43 ^{1} 16.
δύο 41 ^{1B} iii 10.

ἑαυτόν 41 ^{1C} ii 12 *see* αὑτοῦ.
ἐγώ 40 ^{1} 14, ^{2} i 19, 23, ii 7 41
   ^{1A} i [7?], [27?], ^{1B} ii 18, ^{1C} ii

2?, 4, 6, 8, 9 42 ^{1} 10 43 ^{8}
   ii 3, ^{11} 1?, 3, ^{17} 1, ^{21} 2.
ἔθειν 40 ^{2} ii 8 41 $^{5(b)}$ 3.
εἰ 43 ^{11} 5, ^{26} 9? 40 Add. ^{4} 6.
εἰδέναι 40 ^{1} 14 41 ^{1B} ii 12 43 ^{8}
   i 9.
εἶναι 37 ^{1} i 14, 22, 26, ii 1, 20, 36
   41 ^{1A} i 4, 19, ii 30, ^{1B} ii 14, ^{1C}
   ii 2, 10 43 ^{8} i 3, 12?
εἰς 37 ^{1} i 26, 32?, ii 17 40 ^{1} 8 41 ^{1C}
   ii 5, $^{5(a)}$ i 10?, ii 4 42 ^{1} 32.
εἶτα 37 ^{1} ii 35 42 ^{1} 26.
ἐκ 37 ^{1} i 23, 25, 26 40 ^{2} ii 9
   41 ^{4} 9 42 ^{1} 5.
ἐκδανείζειν 41 ^{1B} ii 16.
ἐκεῖνος 41 ^{1B} ii 7.
ἕκητι 43 ^{3} 17.
ἐκκλησία 41 ^{1C} ii 5.
ἐκρηγνύναι [43 ^{21} 3].
ἐκτείνειν 40 ^{2} ii 10.
ἐκφάτνισμα 41 +$^{5(b)}$ 4. $^{5(a)}$ 10
ἐλεύθερος 41 ^{1B} ii 2.
ἕλκειν 42 ^{1} 21, 23, 25.
ελομεν 41 ^{1B} iii 26.
ἐν 37 ^{1} i 7, 19 38 i 41 ^{1B} iii 3,
   ^{1C} ii 8?, 10, 14 42 ^{1} 11 43 ^{8}
   ii 6, ^{11} 10?
ἐναργής 43 ^{8} i 4.
ἐναφιέναι 42 ^{1} 28.
ἔνδοξος 37 ^{1} ii 3.
ἕνεκα 41 ^{1C} ii 4.
ἐνέχεσθαι 42 ^{1} 13.
ἐξάγειν 41 ^{1B} ii 4?
ἐξαλείφειν 41 ^{1A} i 18.
ἑξῆς 37 ^{1} i 13 42 ^{1} 26.
ἐξιοῦν 43 ^{8} 13.
ἐοικέναι 43 ^{2} 1, ^{3} 19.
ἐπειδάν [41 ^{1B} ii 2].
ἐπειδή 42 ^{1} 32.
ἐπέρχεσθαι 41 ^{1B} iii 17.
ἐπί 37 ^{1} i 3, 28? 41 ^{1B} ii 8, 9, 12,
   17, $^{5(a)}$ ii 8? 42 ^{1} 15 43 ^{8}
   ii 2.
ἐπίθετον 38 9.
ἐπικαθα[41 $^{5(a)}$ ii 8.
ἐπικαλεῖν [40 ^{1} 15].
ἐπιλήναιος [37 ^{1} i 28?].
ἐπισκοπεῖν 41 ^{4} 10.
ἐπίσταςθαι 40 ^{2} ii 4, 6.
ἐπωφελεῖν 41 ^{1B} ii 10.
ἔραςθαι 43 ^{8} ii 7.
Ἐρατοςθένης 37 ^{1} ii 10, [31?].
ἔργον 43 ^{8} i 8.
ἔριον 37 ^{1} ii 33.
Ἕρμιππος [37 ^{2} 20?].

(-)ἔρχεςθαι 41 ^{1A} i 9.
ἔςχατος 41 ^{1A} i 22, [23].
ἕτερος 41 ^{1A} ii 20, ^{4} 12 42 ^{1} 13.
εὐγενής 41 ^{1B} ii 11.
εὐδοκιμεῖν 37 ^{1} ii 13.
εὐθύς 37 ^{1} ii 20.
Εὔπολις 38 1 41 ^{1A} 1 back.
εὑρίςκειν 41 ^{1A} ii 10.
εὔρυθμος 42 ^{1} 23.
Εὐφρόνιος 37 ^{1} i 23.
εὐωχεῖν 43 ^{11} 2.
ἔχειν 41 ^{4} 16 43 ^{8} i 3, 6, 11, 18?,
   19?, ^{26} 6, ^{31} 3.
ἐχθρ[43 ^{8} i 29.
ἕως 37 ^{1} ii 12 41 ^{1C} ii 5 43 ^{3} 25.

Ζεύς 40 ^{2} i 14 41 ^{1B} iii 14.
ζητεῖν 41 ^{1A} ii 8, (34a, ^{1B} ii 9a,
   20, 23?, iii 10, ^{1C} i 9).

ἤ 41 ^{4} 11.
ἦ 41 ^{1C} ii 8, 9.
ἤδη 42 ^{1} 9.
ἥκειν 42 ^{1} 14.
ἡμιχόριον 41 ^{1B} iii 5, [$^{5(a)}$ i 12?].

θεα[37 ^{1} ii 1.
θέατρον 41 ^{1C} ii 14.
θεός 38 14 43 ^{3} 17, ^{8} ii 5?
θεος[41 ^{1A} ii 28?
θοινᾶν 43 ^{11} 6?
Θυέστης [43 ^{14} 6].
θύρςος 42 ^{1} 12.

ἰέναι 42 ^{1} 22?
ἱερός 43 ^{17} 5.
ἵζειν 37 ^{1} i 6.
ἵνα 37 ^{2} 12 42 ^{1} 22.
Ἱππεῖς 37 ^{1} i 19.
ἴσος 43 ^{3} 24, 24, ^{26} 5.
ἱστάναι 40 ^{2} i 8.
ἰςχάς 42 ^{1} 9, 15.
Ἴων 37 ^{1} i 24.

καθαιρεῖν 42 ^{1} 11.
καθα[ρ- 41 $^{5(a)}$ ii 8?
(-)κάθαρτος [41 $^{5(a)}$ ii 13].
καί 37 ^{1} ii 4, 15 38 10 40 ^{2} i
   10, 15, 25 41 ^{1A} i 13, 23, 30,
   ii 4, 28, ^{1B} ii 4, 7, [12?], 16, 20,
   21, iii 1, ^{4} 7 42 ^{1} 21, 22, 25
   43 ^{1} 13, ^{8} i 5, ii 1, 10, 11.
καιρός 43 ^{11} 10.
καίτοι 43 ^{3} 22.
κακ[43 ^{3} 18, ^{26} 7.

κακός **41** ¹ᴬ ii 21, 35   **43** ⁸ ii 6,
  ¹⁷ 7 [**40** Add. ¹ ii 1?].
Καλ[**41** ¹ᶜ ii 11?
καλεῖν **43** ¹¹ 7.
(-)καλεῖν **41** ⁵⁽ᵃ⁾ ii 4.
καλός **41** ⁴ 15 **43** ¹⁷ 2?
κάπτειν **41** ⁵⁽ᵃ⁾ ii 9.
κατά **42** ¹ 27, 29.
κατα[**41** ⁵⁽ᵃ⁾ ii 5.
καταγελᾶν **41** ¹ᴮ ii 21.
καταθ[**37** ¹ ii 6.
καταλαμβάνειν **41** ¹ᴬ i 9.
καταπαλαίειν **37** ¹ ii 20, 23.
καταπονεῖν **41** ¹ᴬ i 12.
κελεύειν **38** 2, 6 [**43** ⁸ i 17?].
κενός **41** ¹ᴬ ii 9, 12, [13].
κεραννύναι [**37** ² 1, 4].
κέρδος **41** ¹ᶜ ii 4.
κεφαλή **38** 13.
κλαίειν **40** ² i 23.
Κλέων **41** ¹ᴮ iii 19.
κοινός **41** ¹ᴮ iii 3, 7.
κόκκυ **40** ¹ [16], 18.
κολλᾶν **41** ¹ᴬ ii 19.
κόπτειν **41** ¹ᴮ ii 14.
κόραξ (Κ-?) **43** ⁸ ii 5.
κόρη **43** ¹ 4.
Κορίνθιος **41** ⁵⁽ᵃ⁾ ii 2.
κόρος **43** ⁸ ii 12?
κράδη **42** ¹ 9, 15, 18.
κρατ[**43** ²⁶ 9.
Κρατῖνος **38** 10.
κρεμαννύναι **42** ¹ 14.
κρότημα [**43** ²⁶ 5?].
*κυδᾶν **41** ¹ᴮ ii 1.
κυκᾶν **41** ¹ᴮ ii 16.
κύκλος **43** ¹¹ 8?
κύκνος [**37** ¹ i 19].
κύπτειν **41** ¹ᴮ iii 4.
κύρβις **43** ²⁶ 8.
κῶμος **43** ¹ 10?
κωμῳδία **37** ¹ ii 13.
Κῷος **43** ¹ 7.

Λακεδαι[μ- **41** ⁵⁽ᵃ⁾ i 8.
Λακεδαιμόνιος **41** ¹ᴮ iii 6.
Λάμπων **43** ⁸ ii 5.
λεαίνειν **41** ¹ᴬ i 19.
λέγειν [**37** ¹ i 18] ¹ ii 23 [**40** ² i 22,
  ii 8] **41** ¹ᴬ i 29, ii 14, 36, ¹ᴮ ii 1,
  6, 6, [7], 13, 19, iii 5, ¹ᶜ ii 12,
  ⁴ 2, [11?], 14, ⁵⁽ᵃ⁾ ii 8 **42** ¹ 3
  43 ⁸ i 16.
(-)λέγειν **37** ¹ ii 32.
λειψυδρία **37** ¹ i 7.

λέσχη **41** ¹ᶜ ii 13.
λῆμα **43** ³ 21.
Ληναϊκός **37** ¹ i 34, ii [1?], 2, 17.
Λήναιον [**37** ¹ i 28?].
λόγος **37** ¹ i 13 **40** ¹ 12.
λοιπός **37** ¹ i 11.
λούτριον **37** ¹ i 9, 17.
λύειν **41** ¹ᶜ ii 13.
λυπεῖν [**43** ¹¹ 5].
λυσιτελεῖν [**43** ³ 20].
λωποδύτης [**40** ² i 26].

μακρός **41** ⁴ 16 **42** ¹ 5 **43** ⁸ ii 4.
μαλακός **38** 2, 6.
μαλ[[**37** ¹ ii 32?].
Μαρικᾶς **41** ¹ᴬ i back.
μάχη **43** ²⁶ 3.
μέγας **41** ¹ᴬ i 21, [⁶ 12?].
μείζων see μέγας.
μέλας **43** ⁸ i 14.
μελλ[**42** ⁴ 2.
(-)μέλλειν **43** ²⁴ 4.
μέλος **37** ¹ i 24.
μέν **37** ¹ i 21, ii [1], 12   **41** ¹ᴬ ii
  39, ¹ᴮ [ii 20], iii 1, ¹ᶜ ii 14.
Μένανδρος **41** ¹ᴮ ii 14.
μέντοι **42** ¹ 27 [**43** ¹¹ 3].
μέρος **41** ¹ᴮ ii 17.
μετά **37** ¹ i 10 **43** ⁸ ii 7?
μεταλλάccειν **41** ⁴ 12.
μετατιθέναι **41** ¹ᶜ ii 3.
μεταφορά **41** ¹ᴬ i [14], [16].
μέχρι **42** ¹ 29.
μή **40** ² ii 9.
μηδέ **43** ²⁶ 4.
μηδείς **43** ⁸ i 11.
μήν **41** ¹ᶜ ii 8, 9 **43** ⁸ ii 1.
μηχανοποιός **42** ¹ 10, 17.
μιcεῖν **40** ² i 15.
(-)μιcθον[**40** ¹ 20.
μιcθός **43** ⁸ ii 9.
μνημονεύειν [**40** ² i 24].
μόλις **42** ¹ 33.
μόνος **38** 9.
μοχθηρία **42** ¹ 14.
μῦθος **43** ⁸ ii 4?

νάccειν **37** ¹ ii 35.
ναυτικός **41** ¹ᴮ ii 16, 18.
νεανίας **41** ¹ᴮ ii 20.
νεανίσκος **41** ¹ᴮ ii 23.
Νέμεσις **39** 4.
νέος **37** ¹ ii 21.
νή **40** ² i 14 **41** ¹ᴮ iii 14, ⁴ 13.
νικᾶν **41** ¹ᴬ i 2, 3, ¹ᴮ iii 22?

νιν **40** ¹ 8.
νόθος **41** ⁴ 9.
νόμος **43** ⁸ i 12?
νῦν **37** ² 7 **41** ¹ᴬ i 11, 30, ¹ᶜ ii 4,
  43 ³ 23.

ξενικός **43** ⁸ ii 12.
ξενοκ[**40** Add. ¹ ii 9.
ξυλλέγειν **43** ⁸ ii 9.
ξύλον **41** ¹ᴮ ii 14, ¹ᶜ i 10, ii 10.
ξυνεῖναι **41** ¹ᴮ ii 20.
ξυνῆλιξ **41** ⁵⁽ᵃ⁾ i 11.
ξύνθημα **40** ² i 9.

ὀβολός **37** ¹ ii 30.
ὅδε **43** ¹¹ 9?
οἴεσθαι **43** ¹¹ 3.
οἰκ[**41** ¹ᴮ ii 18?
οἰκεῖν **41** ¹ᴮ ii 8.
οἰκία **41** ¹ᴮ ii 7, 8.
οἰκοδομεῖν **43** ⁸ ii 10.
οἰκοδόμημα **41** ¹ᴮ ii 9.
οἷος **41** ¹ᴬ ii 30, ¹ᴮ ii 12 **42** ¹ 23.
οἰcνουργός **41** ⁴ 13.
ὀλιγο[**37** ¹ ii 27.
ὀλίγος **43** ⁸ ii 13.
ὅλος **41** ¹ᴬ i 29 **43** ⁸ i 11.
Ὅμηρος **37** ¹ i 26.
ὄνομα [**40** ¹ 14].
ὁπότε **42** ⁴ 2.
ὅπως **37** ¹ i 6 **43** ²⁶ 4.
ὁρᾶν **41** ¹ᴮ ii 10, ¹ᶜ ii 9 **43** ⁸ i 5,
  9, ii 6.
ὀρειβατεῖν **41** ¹ᴮ ii 13.
ὀρθός **43** ⁸ i 11.
ὅς **37** ¹ i 3 **42** ¹ 5, 12.
ὅσος **41** ¹ᴮ ii 20.
ὅσπερ **40** ² i 21.
ὅστις **41** ⁵⁽ᵃ⁾ ii 3.
ὅταν **41** ¹ᴮ iii 23?
ὅτι **37** ¹ i 22, 23, 25, ii 11, ² 18
  38 13 **41** ¹ᴮ iii 3 **42** ⁴ 2.
οὐ [**37** ¹ i 11] **40** [¹ 13], ² ii 4, 6
  41 ¹ᴬ ii 35?, ¹ᴮ ii 1 **43** 16, 20,
  ⁸ i 9, ii 6.
οὗ **41** ¹ᶜ ii 5.
οὐδέ **43** ⁸ i 9.
οὐδείς **41** ¹ᴬ ii 9, [13] **43** ⁸ i 6.
οὖν **37** ¹ i 12 **38** 7 **40** ² ii 10
  43 ² 1, ⁸ ii 2.
οὖς **41** ¹ᴬ ii 39?
οὗτος [**37** ¹ ii 21, 22, 23] **40** ² i 24
  41 ¹ᴬ i 4, 5, 18, 29, ii 10, 36, ¹ᴮ
  ii 9, 11, 16, iii 4.
οὕτω(c) **41** ¹ᴬ i 20 **42** ¹ 4, 19.

ὕμνος **37** ¹ i 27.
ὑπαλλαγή **41** ⁴ 17.
ὑπέρ **41** ¹ᴮ ii 13.
ὑπέρα **42** ¹ 22, 26.
Ὑπέρβολος **41** [¹ᴮ iii 4?], ¹ᶜ ii 7, 12.
ὑπό **37** ¹ i 20, ii 24   **41** ¹ᴮ ii 13?, ⁷ ii 6?
ὑποτροπάζειν **41** ¹ᴬ i 7, [8].

φαίνειν **43** ⁸ i 4.
(-)φαίνειν **43** ¹ 1.
φακός [**37** ² 6, 8, 9, 10].
φάναι **37** ² 3   **41** ¹ᴬ i 12?, ⁴ 8   **42** ¹ 25.
φανερός **41** ⁴ 3.
φέρειν **37** ¹ i 11   **41** ¹ᴮ ii 10   **43** ¹¹ 8.
φθέγγεςθαι **41** ¹ᴬ i 20, 21?
φθορά [**40** ¹ 8].
φιλόμολπος **37** ¹ ii 18.

Φοίνιςςαι **42** ¹ 11.
φοιτᾶν **42** ¹ 33.
Φορμίων **40** ¹ 15, ² i 16.
φρενοβλαβής [**41** ⁵⁽ᵃ⁾ i 13].
φρόνηςις **43** ⁸ i 3.
φρυα[**41** ⁵⁽ᵃ⁾ ii 11.
φύειν **43** ⁸ i 7.
φυλακή **40** ² i 18.
φύλλον **43** ⁸ ii 1?

]χαιρ.[**41** ⁸ 2.
χάριν **43** ¹¹ 2?
χάρις **43** ¹¹ 2?
χείρων [**41** ¹ᴬ i 8].
χερα[**43** ²⁵ 4.
χολή **43** ⁸ i 14.
χορευτής **42** ¹ 30.
χορός **37** ¹ i 27, ² 13   **41** ¹ᴬ i 29, ¹ᴮ ii 19, iii 23, ¹ᶜ ii 13.
χρῆμα **43** ⁸ ii 8.

χρῆναι **37** ¹ i 27 **42** ¹ 17 **43** ¹¹ 9.
χρῆςθαι **41** ⁴ 17.
χρόνος **41** ¹ᴬ i 13, 17.
χρυςίον **41** ⁴ 7.
χρυςοκόμης **37** ii 18.
χωρίς [**40** ² i 20?].

(-)ψοφεῖν **43** ¹⁰ 3?
ψυχ[**43** ³ 28.
ψυχρός **42** ¹ 26.

ὦ **41** ⁵⁽ᵃ⁾ i 13 **43** ¹¹ 6?
ὥριος **43** ¹⁷ 2?
ὡς **37** ¹ ii 19 **38** 7 **40** ² i 26 **41** ¹ᴬ ii 38? **42** ¹ 10, 18 **43** ¹¹ 3 **40** Add. ¹ ii 8.
ὡςανεί **42** ¹ 24.
ὥςπερ **41** ¹ᴮ iii 21 **42** ¹ 15.
ὥςτε **43** ⁸ ii 10.
ὠφελεῖν **41** ¹ᴮ ii 21.

(c) COMMENTARY ON UNKNOWN TEXT (2744)

ἄγριος **44** i 1, [5].
αἰςθητικός **44** ii 27.
αἰτία **44** ii 23.
ἀλλά **44** i 6, ii 2.
Ἀλέξανδρος **44** ii 17.
ἄλλος **44** ii 18.
Ἀμερίας **44** ii 11.
ἀνήρ **44** i 5.
Ἀπορήματα **44** ii 23.
Ἀριστοτέλης **44** ii 22.
Ἀριστοφάνης **44** ii 3.
αὐτός **44** ii [4], 31.

*βολαῖα **44** ii 6.
βολεών **44** ii [9], 19.
βορβορώδης [**44** ii 7].

γε **44** i 5.
γῆ **44** ii 1.
γίνεςθαι **44** i 6.

δέ **44** i 7, 37, ii 6, 10, 12, 20, [27].
Δείναρχος **44** ii 12.
δένδρον **44** ii 2.
δηλοῦν **44** ii 21.
διά **44** i 7, ii 24, 25, 27.
διακεῖςθαι [**44** ii 28?].
διαπιαίνειν **44** ii 9?
διατρίβειν **44** ii 21.
διαφθείρειν **44** ii 31.

δραχμή **44** ii 16.
δύναςθαι **44** ii 6.
δυςώδης **44** ii 25.

εἶναι **44** i [8], ii 27.
εἰς **44** i 9.
εἶτα **44** i 9.
ἐκ **44** ii 18.
ἐκθλίβειν [**44** i 10].
ἐκτομίας **44** i 7.
ἐμπίπτειν **44** i 8.
ἐν **44** ii 4, 12, 20, 23.
ἐνταῦθα **44** ii 15.
ἐοικέναι **44** i 5.
ἐπί **44** ii 1, 2, [2].
ἐπορνύναι **44** i 4.
ἑπτακόςιοι **44** ii 15.
Εὐρυςάκειον **44** ii 14.
ἔχειν **44** ii 26.

ἤ **44** ii 25.

καί **44** ii 3, 10, 18, 22, 22, 26, 31, 32, 38.
κακοποιός **44** ii 8.
καλεῖν **44** [i 38], ii 11.
κατά **44** ii 12.
κνιςμός [**44** ii 8].
κοινός **44** i 16?
κοπρεών **44** ii 10.

κόπρος **44** ii 16.
κτᾶςθαι **44** ii 19.

λέγειν **44** ii 5.

μάλιστα **44** ii 8.
μήποτε **44** ii 3.

νέος **44** i 7.
νόςημα **44** i 8.
νοττεύειν [**44** ii 1].

ξύειν **44** i 9.

οἶνος [**44** ii 30].
οἰνόφλυξ [**44** ii 29].
Οἷον **44** ii 18.
Ὅμηρος **44** i 3.
ὄνομα **44** ii 13.
Ὄρνιθες **44** ii 4.
ὄρχις **44** i 9.
ὅς **44** ii 17.
ὀςμή **44** ii 29, [31].
ὅτι **44** ii 20.
οὐ **44** ii 26, 27.
οὐδέ **44** i 5.
οὔτε **44** ii 1, 2.
οὗτος **44** ii [14].
οὕτως **44** ii 24.

πλατύς **44** ii 25.

ποιεῖν **44** i 3.
Πολύευκτος **44** ii 13.
πρός **44** ii 29.
προστιθέναι **44** ii 23.

ῥίον **44** i 6.

ςαπρός **44** ii 32.
ςιτοφάγος [**44** i 5].
ςῦς **44** i 4.

ταῶς **44** ii 6.

τέτραξ **44** ii 5, [5].
τέτριξ **44** i 20.
τίς **44** ii 24.
τοιοῦτος **44** ii 20, 32.
τόπος **44** ii 7, 21.
*τραξ (τραγα P. = οὔραγα Aristot. *Hist. an.* 559ᵃ11 seq.) **44** ii 1?

ὑλήεις **44** i 6.
ὑπέρ **44** ii 16.

φάναι **44** ii 11, 17.
φαῦλος [**44** ii 30?].

χαίρειν **44** ii 25.
χαλεπός [**44** i 2].
χαμαίζηλος **44** ii 3.
χλούνης **44** i 4.
χρῆςθαι **44** ii 13.

ὥςπερ **44** i 3, [ii 29].

PLATE I

PLATE II

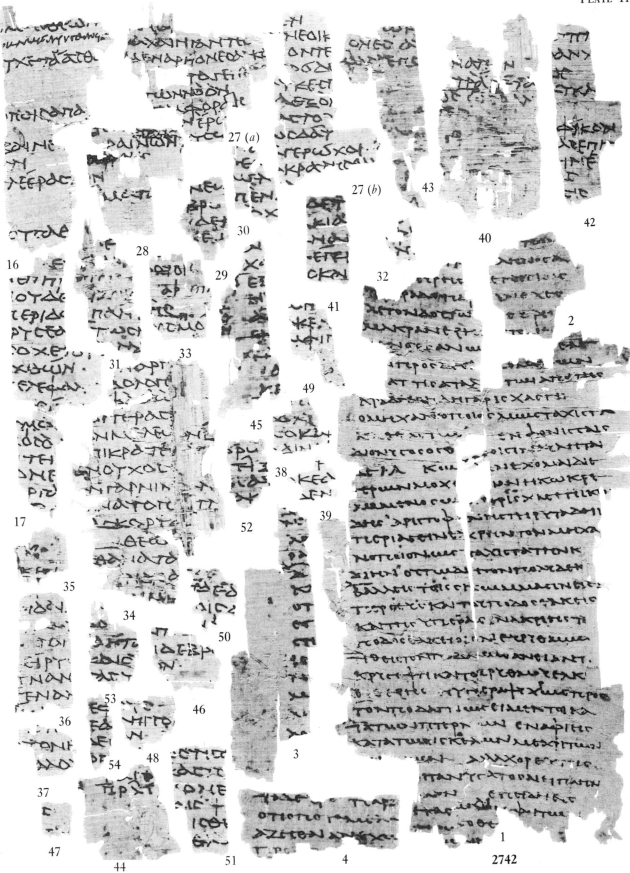

27 (a)

27 (b)

43

42

40

30

16   28

29   32   2

41

31   33   49

45

17   38

52   39

35

34

50

53   46

36

54   48

37

47

44   51   4   1

2735   2742

PLATE III

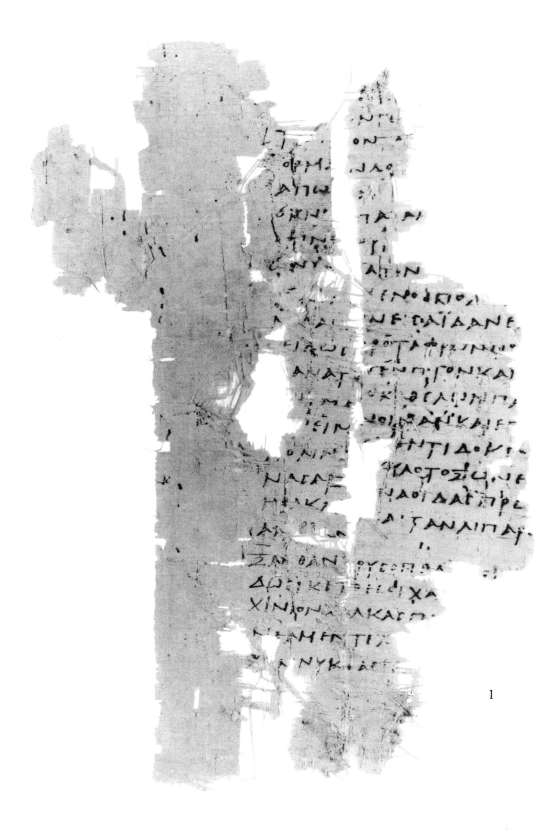

1

2736

PLATE IV

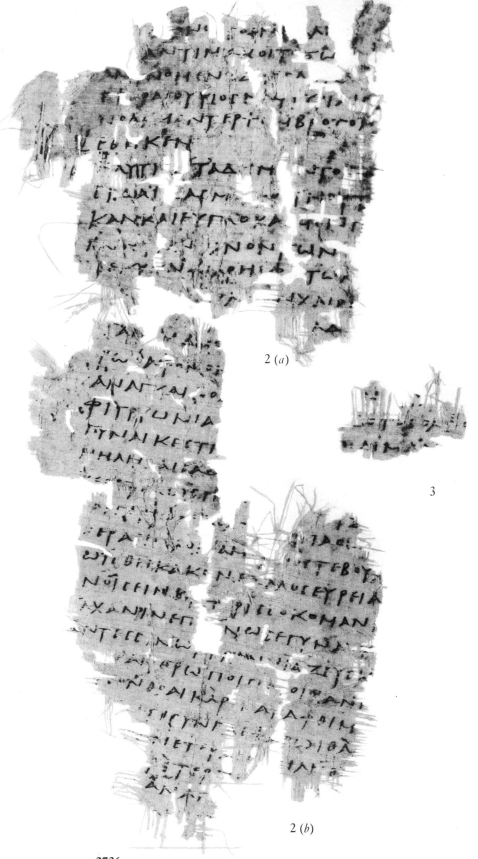

2 (a)

3

2 (b)

2736

PLATE V

1

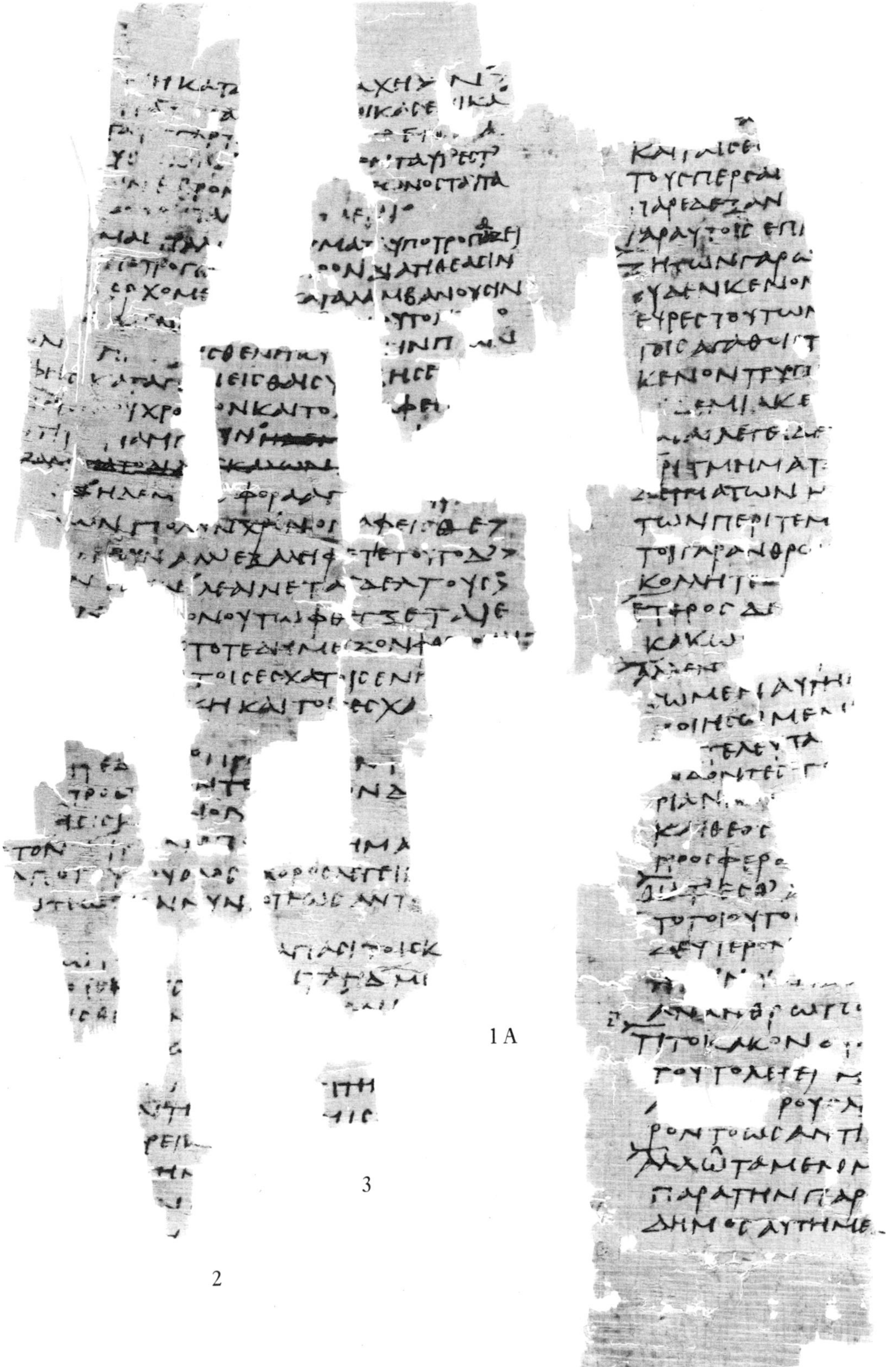

PLATE VI

1 A

3

2

PLATE VIII

11

12

10

6

7

8

9

2

2737

4

2741

PLATE IX

1

2

3

1

8

9 (a)

9 (b)

2

2740 Add.

2740

PLATE X

4

5

7

2733

6

2740 Add.

2739

2738

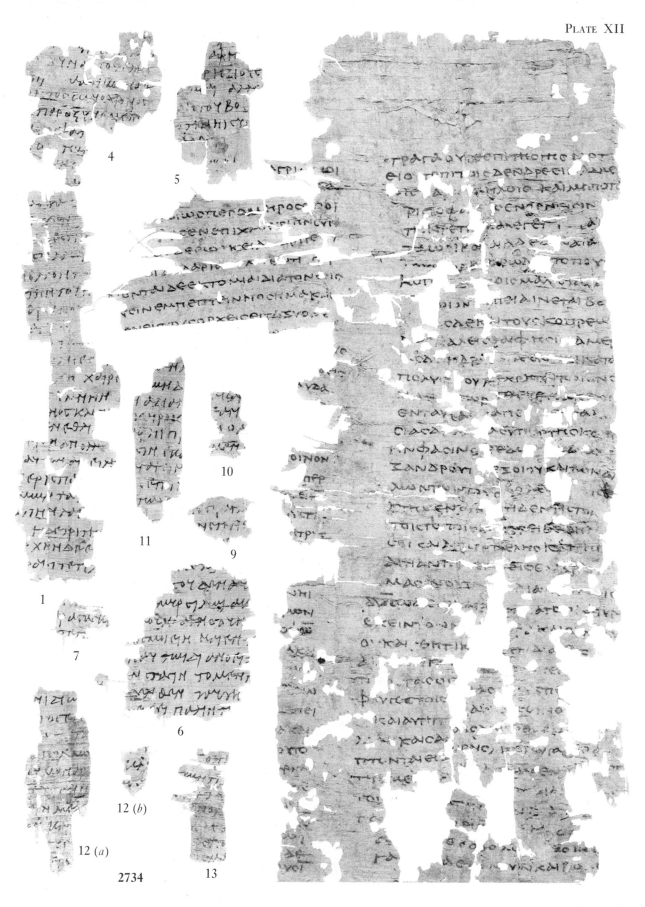

PLATE XII

4

5

10

11

9

1

7

6

12 (b)

12 (a)

2734

13

2744